"Perfect for any kid who wants to know the what, why, and how behind staying healthy. Dr. Nina Shapiro is more than a beloved doctor, she's become a leading voice in translating complicated medical information into accessible, actionable advice. Now she's done it again, this time for kids!"

—**Cara Natterson, MD,** *New York Times* **bestselling author of The Care and Keeping of You and the Guy Stuff series**

"This book empowers kids to learn about their bodies and take charge of their health . . . and will probably teach their parents a few things, too!"

—**Ari Brown, MD, bestselling author of the Baby 411 series**

"In engaging and child-friendly language, Dr. Nina Shapiro describes how the human body works, how to take care of it, and why it's essential to do so. This excellent book teaches elementary-aged children how their bodies work while giving parents a welcome primer that answers their questions. I wish I had this book on my shelf when my kids were growing up!"

—**Susan Kaiser Greenland, bestselling author of** *The Mindful Child* **and Mindful Games**

"*The Ultimate Kids' Guide to Being Super Healthy* is an accessible health manual for kids of any age. . . . Dr. Shapiro offers detailed information in an easy-to-read guide while keeping the tone of this book supportive, flexible, and fun. All kids—and their parents, too!—can learn something from this book."

—Charlotte H. Markey, PhD, professor of psychology, Rutgers University and author of *The Body Image Book for Girls* and *The Body Image Book for Boys*

"This guide is exactly what every kid asks, with answers every parent wants to know. From snacks to screens, sleep to shots, and everything in between, Dr. Nina Shapiro makes it super easy to be super healthy. She covers it all in this fun, fact-filled, easy-to-read and hard-to-argue-about guide that kids (and parents!) will enjoy."

—Tanya Altmann, MD, FAAP, pediatrician, award-winning and bestselling author of *What to Feed Your Baby*

"Using her warm, down-to-earth, and often humorous style, Dr. Nina Shapiro gives kids the real answers that parents often lack in responding to 'Whyyyyyyy' when it comes to self-care. How I wish I had this book when I was raising my kids! It is invaluable and essential to every parent's and child's library for reference over and over again."

—Betsy Brown Braun, child development and behavior specialist, bestselling author of *Just Tell Me What to Say* and *You're Not the Boss of Me*

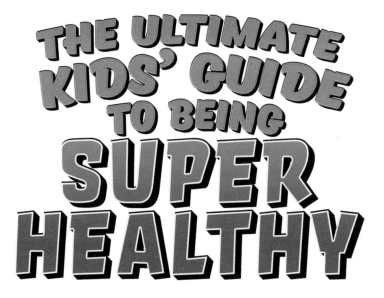

THE ULTIMATE KIDS' GUIDE TO BEING SUPER HEALTHY

WHAT YOU NEED TO KNOW ABOUT NUTRITION, EXERCISE, SLEEP, HYGIENE, STRESS, SCREEN TIME, AND MORE

NINA L. SHAPIRO, MD
ILLUSTRATIONS BY NICOLE GRIMES

Sky Pony Press
New York

This book is designed to increase knowledge, awareness, and understanding of how kids can better learn about their bodies and how they can stay as healthy as they can. It's also designed to be fun—so that kids and adults can see how cool science of health can be.

It is not intended to replace the advice that your or your child's physician can provide.

Library of Congress Cataloging-in-Publication Data is available on file.

Cover design by Brian Peterson
Cover illustrations by Nicole Grimes

Print ISBN: 978-1-5107-6493-4
Ebook ISBN: 978-1-5107-6495-8

Printed in China

For AIA and CMA.
And for all of the kids who teach grown-ups every day.

CONTENTS

A NOTE TO GROWN-UPS

Since time immemorial, children have been programmed to listen to and heed the rules that adults make:

"Clean your room!"

"Time for bed!"

"Turn off your screen!"

"Eat your vegetables!"

By the time a child is five years old, they have heard no fewer than five thousand requests, demands, limits, and nonnegotiable orders. If today's kids were able to understand why they have to do what they do for their health and well-being, they may grow up to be a generation of healthier beings who understand why they eat vegetables, why they need to get to sleep, and why they need to take medicine (or, perhaps more importantly, why they need to NOT take medicine). The science of the workings of the human body can be cool, and it can actually be simplified to the degree that a young child can understand it. If a child can visualize what goes on inside their body, and how their world affects their body, using real words and real science, then eating, sleeping, taking medicines, and even getting shots will take on whole new meanings.

Nutrition and diet are a central focus of many parents and caregivers. If the adults start their kids early—give them green vegetables, healthy proteins, and minimize fat and sugar intake—then, by force of habit, kids continue these practices through older childhood into adulthood, right? Alas, exposure by peers, media, and well-meaning school lunch programs will quash those plans before a child hits the first or second grade. Ask the average (or even above-average) eight-year-old why they should limit their sugar intake and perhaps eat more protein, fruits, and vegetables, and you may get such answers as "Sugar makes me hyper," "Spinach makes you strong," "Meat has protein." It's likely that the average thirty-eight-year-old won't have much more in-depth understanding of nutrition, either.

While the science behind health is a complex array of variables, mind-numbing data, and nearly incomprehensible biochemical cascades, the vast majority of the explanations to health maintenance can be remarkably simple. Even when not so simple, the important issues can be simplified so the average elementary school student can understand.

Imagine if every second grader knew what REM sleep was, knew what happens to their brain when watching a screen, and understood why fruit juice is nowhere nearly as healthy as fruit. This is possible! In *The Ultimate Kids' Guide to Being Super Healthy*, I ask children (and adults!) to embark on an amazing journey through their body, as it's getting fed, protected, exercised, and rested. Using illustrative, simple, yet accurate science encourages and enables kids to take control of their health from all vantage points. The language will be age-appropriate, and the voice will be geared toward children in kindergarten through fifth grade.

In *The Ultimate Kids' Guide To Being Super Healthy*, each chapter provides children with age-appropriate explanations and illustrations about how foods affect different organs in both short- and long-term ways, what their body does when they run, sleep, or use an electronic device, how medicines and immunizations work, and much more. While the book is designed with a young reader in mind, it's also meant to be read together with an adult, especially with one who's also interested in a little brush-up on how the body works! In fact, I hope that this book will spark interest in the science behind health on the part of both kids and adults. If a topic is of particular interest to you or your child, there are so many great books, videos, in-person professionals, websites, and educational programs to keep the passion for science going.

Here we go!

INTRODUCTION

Welcome to *The Ultimate Kids' Guide To Being Super Healthy*! We are about to go on the most amazing journey. Why is it so amazing? Because it's a journey all about YOU.

You've done a lot of great things in your life every day since the day you were born without even knowing how great they are. You eat yummy food, you sleep and have some cool dreams (or maybe even some scary dreams, too), you play indoors, you play outside, you learn, you grow, you go to doctor and dentist check-ups, and sometimes, on not such good days, you get sick.

I'll bet a lot of your days and nights are spent listening to grown-ups. They tell you what to eat, when to eat, when to sleep, when to wake up, and even when and where to play. What is it about all these grown-ups and their bossiness?

Well, believe it or not, grown-ups are telling you what to do because they are hoping for you to be healthy, happy, and well-balanced in your world. As you get older, they may give you more and more chances to make decisions, but I'd guess right now they're still calling most of the shots.

Wouldn't it be great if you had a better understanding of why your grown-ups are making so many demands of you? Is there any real logic to what they're saying? I bet you'd love it if they let you have cookies and ice cream for dinner, let you stay up as late as you wanted, didn't make you wash your hands (with soap) so many times each day, and never ever brought you to the doctor's office to get a shot. Well, it sure would be a fun few days, weeks, or months, but deep down, you probably already know that you would end up feeling pretty crummy—and definitely not healthy.

We're about to take a journey into your world—we'll see what happens to your body when you eat and drink, when you play, when you sleep, when you learn, when you stay clean, when you relax, and when you need to see your doctor. I promise that while we're on our adventure, and after our adventure as well, you will see your world differently. So much will make so much more sense. And I also promise that you will very likely be able to teach your grown-ups a few things about what you've learned. (They don't know *everything*, after all. But sshhh—don't tell them I said that.)

So, sit back or stand, buckle up or jump up and down, and enjoy the ride! Feel free to bring a friend, sibling, or grown-up along the way!

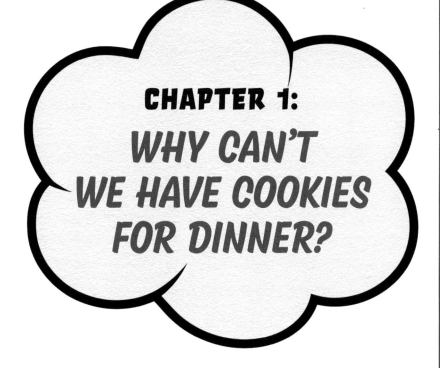

CHAPTER 1:

WHY CAN'T WE HAVE COOKIES FOR DINNER?

Why in the world CAN'T we have cookies for dinner? I'm going to let you in on a fun fact many people don't know: most adults don't know the answer to this! And if an adult is reading this with you, I bet they're just as interested to find out the answer as you! You may both even be thinking the same thing: *Cookies for dinner sounds like a great idea!* Okay, maybe it does, but first let's see what's in a cookie.

If you've baked them from scratch, or even from a mix, you might have a rough idea. To make cookies, you need flour, sugar (LOTS of sugar), eggs, baking soda,

butter, some flavoring, and any extra treats, like chocolate chips, nuts, or raisins.

Well, that doesn't seem so bad! Flour is in just about everything, including bread and pasta. Sugar is yummy, and eggs are good for you. Baking soda is just something usually buried deep in the kitchen cabinet so who knows what that's for, but it's only like a teaspoon so what's the difference, right? Butter, just like milk, is from a cow. Treats like raisins and nuts are pretty healthy. Now that you mention it, maybe we should have cookies for dinner!

Not so fast.

Don't get me wrong. Cookies are yummy and great, and cookies made from scratch have some pretty healthy ingredients. But your body needs even MORE good stuff to help you grow, be strong, feel good, have long lasting energy, and be able to focus at school.

First, let's talk about where food goes once you eat it. The process is called **DIGESTION**, and it's pretty cool. Digestion is the breaking apart of the foods you eat—

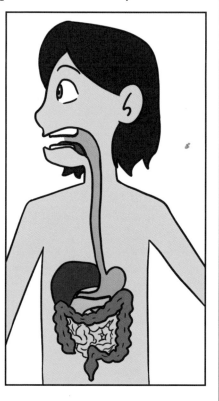

separating the healthy substances from the useless substances that become waste (more on that further down, literally). Digestion also helps the good stuff you eat and drink get to where it needs to go—all over your body—your muscles, your internal organs, your brain, your heart, your skin, and even your eyes.

After you eat or drink something and chew and swallow it, it moves from your mouth down a very floppy muscle-lined tube (as floppy as the inner tube of a bicycle tire without any air in it) called the **ESOPHAGUS**. Your **SALIVA** (otherwise known as your "spit") contains materials called **ENZYMES**, which help start the digestion of your food, even before the food leaves your mouth.

Enzymes are substances in your body that help turn bigger parts of the food you eat into smaller and smaller pieces. These pieces become so tiny thanks to the enzymes that eventually you can't even see them! They need to be really tiny to travel to all the different parts of your body.

Your teeth help with digestion, too, by breaking pieces of food into smaller and smaller pieces. The esophagus helps push the food from your mouth to your **STOMACH**, which is a small pouch about the size of your fist. When you point to your "stomach" or have a "stomach ache," you're probably pointing to your whole belly area. Your *actual* stomach is only a small part of that!

While your teeth and saliva help get the digestion process started, your stomach does a lot more work in that area. It contains MORE enzymes to break up the food particles, and it acts as a squeezing bag to break down the food to even smaller pieces.

Here's a fun thing to try:

(And if your grown-up gets angry, you can blame me on this one.)

(On second thought, do it WITH your grown-up! They'll need to do the knife work.)

TRY THIS! ACTIVITY

Take a plastic bag and fill it with some fresh blueberries, bananas, and strawberries, or any other berries you might have on hand. Take another bag and fill it with a few pieces of chopped apples (with the peels still on) and oranges. Give each bag a few good squeezes. Really get in there! Use two hands!

Guess what?

You just did the same job your stomach does!

Take a look at both bags. Do they look and feel different now? The one with the berries and bananas may be a big mush (it's yummy to eat, and you can even blend it into a smoothie), and the one with apples and oranges has a lot more pieces left over (you can add these to your smoothie, as well. Yum!). This is because apple peel and orange slices have a lot of **FIBER**.

Fiber is a really important substance in many foods that helps with digestion because it doesn't fall apart. It helps move the unnecessary stuff you eat (yes, that you'll eventually poop out) through your body. It moves along the whole digestive system, even past the stomach. It doesn't get absorbed but helps pull out the waste materials.

The other great thing about fiber is that it slows down your digestion. I know you may often be told to "hurry up!" but when it comes to certain things, slow is the best way to go. If your digestion can slow down a bit, the energy that you need from foods will last much longer. This is one of the many reasons why whole fruits, even berries and bananas, which may turn to mush in your plastic-bag-stomach creation, get digested much more slowly than fruit juices or sweetened drinks of any kind. Other foods with a lot of fiber include broccoli, cauliflower, celery, dark green lettuce, and most raw fruits and vegetables. The fiber in these do wonders for your digestion.

Onward past the stomach!

Next your food mush (and hopefully some fiber) goes to your **INTESTINES**. First it goes to your **SMALL INTESTINES**, and then to your **LARGE INTESTINES**. If you've ever seen a drawing of someone's insides, the intestines are the long squiggly tubes in your belly. The funny thing is that the small intestines are much much MUCH bigger (well, longer) than your large intestines. In grown-ups, small intestines can be up to twenty-two feet long! That's like the length of about three grown-ups plus one first-grader standing on top of one another!

The small intestines are called "small" because they are narrow, about one inch wide, as opposed to the large intestines, which are wider, about three inches wide. And large intestines, which wrap around the outside of the small intestines, are about five feet long, or the height of one small adult (like me!).

Your intestines do a whole lot more than just let the mushed-up food pass along through those nearly thirty feet of squiggly tubes on a wild ride like an amusement

22 ft

park water slide. They are also busy pushing the food along, but most importantly, they act to let the good parts of the foods you eat (like the **VITAMINS**, **MINERALS**, **PROTEINS**, **FATS, WATER**, and **CARBO- HYDRATES**) get absorbed into your body. (We'll talk about all these good parts in a bit.) This works because the insides of your intestines are lined with tiny little hair- like bumps, almost like the

7

yarn of a shaggy carpet. Each of these tiny (and when I say tiny, I mean *tiny!* About one millimeter long, or the length of a tiny ant) "hairs," called **VILLI**, help absorb nutrients into your bloodstream and then all over your body. The downside is that they also absorb the not-so-healthy stuff, which also goes to your bloodstream and all over your body.

After everything is absorbed into your bloodstream, both good and bad, the remainder of your food is known as **WASTE**. Yup, that's right, when you feel the need to poop, that solid brown stuff is what's left of the food you ate and some of the drinks you drank, anywhere from half a day to two days before you poop them out.

So now you have a pretty good idea about how the food gets from your mouth to the, well, end, known as your rectum and your anus, and that a lot of the broken-up parts get into your body. And that some of it goes out as waste. But let's get back to that question of cookies!

Why is it better to, say, have some protein-containing food like meat, chicken, fish, eggs, soy, cheese, nuts or beans, AND some fiber-and vitamin-containing food like vegetables, AND just small amounts of foods like butter or bread, than it is to eat ONLY delicious cookies?

The answer lies in HOW these foods are digested, WHAT they become when they're broken down by those enzymes of yours, HOW LONG they take to get through your body, and HOW MUCH energy they will give you and for how long. A lot happens to your food between your mouth and the end of your intestines, and a lot of what happens occurs outside of the main organs we just talked about.

The main ingredients in cookies are flour and sugar. Flour is used for baking cookies, cakes, breads, crackers, chips, and pastas. While there are many types of flour (white flour, wheat flour, and more), all flour contains **STARCH**. Starch is a type of carbohydrate.

CARBOHYDRATES are substances that are really important in our diet. They give us energy. They contain several **ELEMENTS**, including **CARBON**, **HYDROGEN**, and **OXYGEN**. Some carbohydrates are made up of many carbons, hydrogens, and oxygens, and these are known as complex carbohydrates (starches). Other carbohydrates, such

as white flour, and, yes, sugar, only have a few carbons, hydrogens, and oxygens, and these are known as simple carbohydrates (sugars). The more complex the carbohydrate, the longer it takes to break up into the simple carbohydrates (sugars), and the longer they'll take to digest.

But remember, slower digestion can be a good thing! The longer something takes to digest, or break up into smaller pieces, the longer lasting your energy will be. Cookies, which have lots of simple carbohydrates, will be digested quickly. You'll get a quick burst of energy, and then be hungry again before you know it. If you eat something that's a complex carbohydrate, like wheat bread, brown rice, whole fruits (these can be fresh or frozen), or sweet potatoes, it takes a much longer time to turn them into a simple carbohydrate, better known as sugar. The longer it takes for something to turn into sugar through digestion, the longer your energy will last from eating it!

While a little sugar, breads, pastas, and crackers are fine in your diet, your body recognizes all of these as simple, quick, short-lasting energy sources. The sugar in them gets absorbed into your bloodstream and goes to an organ called your **LIVER**. If there's a lot of sugar in your liver, some of that sugar can actually be turned into fat. Another organ called the **PANCREAS** also acts to connect with all that sugar by releasing a **HORMONE** called **INSULIN**. The substance insulin helps store energy and is released from your pancreas in very high amounts if you eat a lot of sugar. If there's a lot of insulin roaming around in your body, it sends a signal to your brain (yes, all the way from your belly to your brain!) saying, "Hey, you're not full! You're still hungry!" It's tricking your brain into thinking that you need more to eat, even if you've had enough. Especially if that "enough" had a lot of sugar.

Other foods take slightly different paths in your digestion. Fruits and vegetables are made of mostly water. Yes, even less liquidy fruits like bananas have a lot of water in them. If you take the water out of any fruit, they shrivel down to a fraction of their original size. That's why dried fruits, like raisins (which are dried grapes), dried apricots, or dried figs are so much smaller than the fresh versions. All the water's been taken out! When you eat a whole fruit (well, you don't have to eat the *whole* fruit, especially if we're talking about a whole watermelon or a whole pineapple), you chew it up, and most of it eventually turns into water in your stomach and intestines.

This water, much needed for your body to stay **HYDRATED**, gets absorbed into your bloodstream in your small and large intestines. Some of it gets filtered in another organ called your **KIDNEYS**. Most people have two kidneys, but some have only one, which is just fine, too. The kidneys filter out any substances in your bloodstream that you don't need. They help turn the liquid waste materials into **URINE** (otherwise known as pee), which gets stored in your bladder until you pee it out. Yes, urine is just diluted, filtered blood! But there's no blood in your urine. At least there shouldn't be.

The rest of the vegetables and fruits are the fiber. Good old fiber, your friend, helps slow down the absorption of sugar from the fruits into your blood stream and helps take along all of your other food waste in the journey through your intestines. The other good parts of fruits and vegetables—vitamins and minerals—travel along into your bloodstream and body along with the water they contain.

PROTEIN-containing foods like meats, eggs, dairy products like milk and cheese, and vegetable proteins like soy and beans, take a bit of a different path than fruits, vegetables, or starches and sugars. Many of these foods contain several parts, including the protein part, as well as some fat and, in the case of vegetable proteins like beans and soy, our friend fiber.

You may have heard people (usually grown-ups!) say things like "Protein builds muscle!" or "Milk makes strong bones!" There's a bit of truth to these! Proteins are substances made of similar elements we see in carbohydrates—carbon, hydrogen, and oxygen. They also contain the element **NITROGEN**, and sometimes another element called **SULFUR**. These elements link together to form really *really* large clusters of elements called **MOLECULES** that form into proteins. These proteins are what we call the "building blocks" of our **CELLS** and can also give you long-lasting energy and help you grow. When you eat foods with protein, enzymes (remember we talked about these on page 4?) help break these huge protein molecules into smaller pieces.

Enzymes are kind of like soap—when you add soap to a greasy pan, the soap breaks up the grease. When you add enzymes (which you have in your saliva, your stomach, and your intestines), it breaks up proteins into smaller molecules called **AMINO ACIDS**. These amino acids are really important for growing, giving you energy, and even helping you heal if you fall and scrape your knee. (Isn't your body incredible?)

You eat many different types of fats, and most of them are mixed in with other things. These can include butter, margarine, or the fat that's in milk or meats. A little bit of fat in your diet is just fine. There are research scientists and nutrition specialists who spend their workdays trying to figure out which are the "best" and "healthiest" fats to eat. Oils like olive oil, coconut oil, and other vegetable oils are also forms of fats. Fats are made up of really large molecules that need to be made smaller before they get to your bloodstream. As with proteins and carbohydrates, certain types of enzymes in your intestine and other organs help break the fats down into smaller pieces. Fats can often get a bad rap, but they do help you grow and can give you long-lasting energy.

Other nutrients that are really important for your growth are vitamins and minerals. The vitamins in milk are **VITAMINS A AND D**, which help you keep your bones strong and your vision sharp. Milk also contains a **MINERAL** (a substance similar to a vitamin) called **CALCIUM**, which is needed to grow strong bones. Vegetables and fruits, which are mostly water and fiber, also contain a lot of great vitamins. **VITAMIN C**, which is in most fruits and vegetables, helps your body with healing cuts and scrapes and helps you have strong teeth and gums. **FOLATE**, a **B-VITAMIN** in many vegetables, helps strengthen your blood cells. **POTASSIUM**, in fruits like bananas and peaches, makes your heart healthier.

Okay, so maybe it's not the best idea to have cookies for dinner. Yes, they are no doubt super yummy, as are ice cream, cake, candy, and so many other sweet treats.

But now that you know what's in this stuff (mostly sugar and flour), you now know that they don't really give you all the good stuff you need to grow, have energy, and take care of all of the other parts of your body, like your muscles, bones, and heart. They're also not much help to your ability to heal or your ability to create long-lasting energy and growth.

✳

And speaking of energy, you need a lot of it to do fun things like play outside, kick around a soccer ball, go swimming, climb a play structure, or dance all afternoon. These are called exercises, and we'll talk about them next!

CHAPTER 2:
WHAT'S SO GOOD ABOUT EXERCISE?

Are you someone who really likes running around? Do you have a favorite sport to play? Or do you prefer sitting quietly reading a book, doing a puzzle, or (like so many kids!) do you prefer to be on your screen of choice for as long as you're allowed? Some kids like to mix it up and are happy to sit and relax but also love getting outside to play. As a kid (actually, also as an adult), getting outside (or inside if the weather's not great) to run around, swim, climb on play structures, shoot hoops, or participate in any kind of physical activity is part of keeping your body and mind healthy.

Exercise is really REALLY important for you. And the great thing about exercise is that it can and *should* be fun! There is no "best" exercise, so you can just do what you love to do! The only "bad" exercise is something that's dangerous—like riding a bike or a scooter without a helmet, swimming without an adult watching you, or horsing around with a friend at the top of a really high play structure where one or both of you could fall and get badly hurt. Other than doing something unsafe, all exercise is great for you.

Another great thing about exercise is that you can do it pretty much anywhere. And yet ANOTHER great thing about it is that if you do a little bit every day (aim for one hour), you'll feel healthy and strong, you'll sleep better, and even do better in school!

What happens to your body when you exercise? Well, it really depends what kind of exercise you're doing. Are you going for a nice walk in your neighborhood, doing some stretching, or running a race, playing a soccer game, or splashing in the ocean waves?

The first two, walking and stretching, are great for moving your **MUSCLES** and *JOINTS*, and also for feeling good while you're doing them. You may not get out of breath, you may not feel your heart pumping, and you may not even feel tired afterward. That's okay! It's still exercise, and it's still great for you.

It's also really great for you to do something every day that "gets your heart pumping." Okay, okay—your heart is ALWAYS pumping. But it's different when you run around or swim or go on your bike. You might even feel your heart beating, your face may get a little warm or flushed, and you may notice that you're breathing faster. Your heart is a muscle, similar to other muscles in your body. The difference is, you don't have to think about making that muscle work.

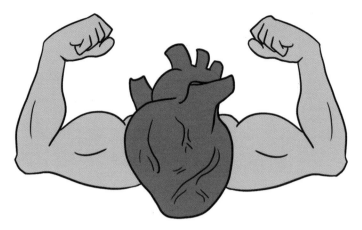

When you kick a ball, swim across a pool, or pump your bike pedals, your brain is (very quickly!) telling those arm, leg, and even **ABDOMINAL** muscles (the muscles in front of your stomach area) to get in gear and work! When your heart works harder, it pumps blood faster and more strongly. It's moving the blood in your body to all those muscles that need extra energy. Just like other muscles in your body, if your heart gets a bit of its own exercise every day, it will be stronger and healthier.

When you're exercising, your breathing may get faster and deeper to help get more air (specifically, oxygen) into your lungs. Your skin may get flushed or feel warm because your blood vessels (the tiny tubes that carry your blood around) get a bit stretched out so that more blood can get to your muscles. It also lets your skin "breathe," opening up some of the **PORES** to let the sweat out!

Are you ever thirsty during or after heavy exercise? This is partly because when you breathe out, you're breathing out some water. Water in your breath? Try fogging up a window or a mirror by breathing hard on it. That spot you just created is water! (Make a smiley face with your finger in your little water spot!)

When you sweat, even if you don't realize you're sweating, your body also releases water that you need to replace by drinking it. That's called staying **HYDRATED**, meaning you have enough water in your body. And if you sweat a lot and don't drink enough liquids, you can get **DEHYDRATED**, meaning you don't have enough water in your body.

The other amazing thing about exercise is that it helps the body even when you're not doing it. If you do a little exercise in the morning, for example, your workout continues to help your muscles, heart, and lungs get strong the rest of the day, long after you've finished running or playing. It helps with other ways you may not have thought about, too—exercising regularly helps you get better sleep, focus better in school, and it even helps your digestion! This is because exercising daily helps with something called your **METABOLISM**.

Your metabolism is the way that you (and only you) keep the inner workings of your body going—your heartbeat, your breathing, your digestion, and your sleep.

Kids and adults who exercise regularly tend to have their best possible metabolism that they can have as individuals. While nobody can fully control their own metabolism (in many ways, it's something you're born with, and it changes as you  get older and older), everyone can play a part in making their metabolism as healthy as they can.

We know there is no "best" exercise, but there are a few things to think about when it comes to what exercise can do for you. The first thing is **ENDURANCE**. There are two types of endurance. The first is endurance of your heart and blood vessels, meaning that the stronger they get from exercise, the more they'll be able to move oxygen and energy through your body. This comes from doing exercise that gets your heart and muscles moving quickly and powerfully.

Activities like running, bike riding, skating, and swimming help your heart and muscles build up endurance.

These are called **AEROBIC** activities. Aerobic means that the activity is moving oxygen around your body. Oxygen is not just in the air—it's also in your blood! It's really important that your blood carries oxygen all over your body. The oxygen that your blood transports to all of your organs helps give them energy and helps your body grow.

The other kind of endurance is for the muscles in your arms, your legs, your back, and your abdomen (your "stomach" area muscles). These aerobic activities help build muscle strength, making it easier and easier to do the activities you love. It may mean that you'll start running faster and feel less tired during and after running. It may be that you'll be able to swim farther, or bike up a steep hill that you had to walk your bike up in the past.

Another thing that exercise can do for you is give you **STRENGTH**. This doesn't mean that you need to be a muscle-bulging body builder. But doing exercises like climbing, hiking, throwing and catching a ball, or doing cartwheels all build strength. The more often you do it, the stronger your muscles can get!

Other really important benefits of exercise are **FLEX-IBILITY** and **BALANCE**. These can come from tumbling, stretching, doing yoga, gymnastics, or dancing. Flexibility means that your joints get easier to bend safely without causing any aches or injuries. These joints are like hinges of a door and can be found between your upper and lower arms (your elbows), upper and lower legs (your knees), your shoulders, your hips, and your neck and back.

Balance is super important and comes from doing exercises that work your balance, like tumbling, bike riding, skating, skateboarding, and dancing or yoga. The more you practice balance activities, the better your balance will get, and the more fun these types of activities will become.

Let's take a look at bike riding. If you're learning to ride a bicycle, which involves aerobic activity (endurance), flexibility, strength, and balance, it's not a whole lot of fun if you feel wobbly every time your feet leave the ground and hit those pedals. But if you've already learned to ride a bike, with either two wheels or four wheels, you might remember that feeling when it no longer was a struggle but became fun! Maybe you pedaled away from your grown-up or older sibling, who had been holding the back of your bicycle seat, and felt that

wind at your sides and felt a bit of speed as you took off down the street on your own. Maybe you wanted to bike over and over again, every day, after you really got the hang of it.

But before you got to that point, it might have felt scary, like a lot of work, and definitely not a lot of fun. Sometimes once you learn something like bike riding, you quickly forget how hard it was to learn! The nice thing about bike riding in particular is that once you learn, you never forget this great skill. Adults even use the expression "It's like riding a bicycle" when they're talking about something that they may not have done in a long time but can pick up right away without having to learn it all over again.

A similar challenge comes with learning to swim. So many kids don't like those first times in the water. They don't like getting water on their face, in their ears, or in their eyes. Some find that learning to swim is really scary.

And definitely not a lot of fun. Maybe this is sounding very familiar. Maybe you're going through this right now! Or maybe a younger sibling or a friend is really not liking the whole swimming thing. Well, if it's you, or if it's a friend or family member, be patient. Learning to swim is a really important skill to master. But for some, it takes more time than for others. Some kids are like "fish" and take to the water before they even learn to walk. Some may take years to overcome fears and worries. And that's okay, too.

There is no perfect way to learn to swim. But the best recommendation I have is to find a teacher—whether it's a parent, relative, friend, neighbor, or professional swim teacher—who knows how to teach safe swimming. For instance, while it's really great to learn how to go under water, I think you'd agree that it's even more important to learn to come up to the surface to get air after being under water! So, let's first talk about swimming for safety.

Why would you need to learn to swim for safety if you don't want to go swimming? Well, the world has lots of water in it. There are oceans, lakes, rivers, ponds, and some really big puddles! And, of course, there are swimming pools and even bathtubs! If you're on a boat, at a beach, or at a home with a pool, even if you don't choose to go in the water, you may accidentally fall in, so it's important to know how to swim!

Okay, we got that out of the way.

Swimming for safety is a skill, but swimming for fun is, well, fun! Once you do learn how to swim, it's a great time. It's one of the best exercises, because it includes all of what we just talked about—endurance, strength, flexibility, and balance. You use all of your muscles when you swim without putting too much strain on your joints, as you would with running, soccer, or basketball. And swimming can take on so many forms—splashing in the ocean, riding the waves, body surfing, surfboarding, or boogie boarding. Swimming laps in a pool, learning how to jump or dive, tumbling in the water, or playing pool games like diving for rings or playing water polo. Snorkeling in the sea or learning how to water ski or wakeboard.

Most kids who learn to swim *love* to swim. It just takes more time for some to learn than others. If you're one of those slower swimmers, don't give up. Give yourself time. You'll be even prouder when you learn how to do it. If your friend or sibling is a struggling swimmer, but you're a superstar in the pool, be patient with them. It comes naturally to some, but not to all. Keep encouraging them and supporting even the littlest bit of progress. That will keep them trying, and someday they'll get it, too.

No matter the sport, or form of exercise, doing so many kinds of activities really does wonders for your body. Even if you don't feel tired at the end of the day after you exercised, people who exercise every day actually get a better night's sleep. And if you get a good night's sleep, you'll have better days. You'll be sharper at school, in a better mood, and guess what? You'll have more energy to exercise again!

✳

Speaking of getting a good night's sleep, stay tuned for why that's so important, and why an early bedtime might not be as bad as it sounds. (It's okay to roll your eyes. I know what you're thinking!)

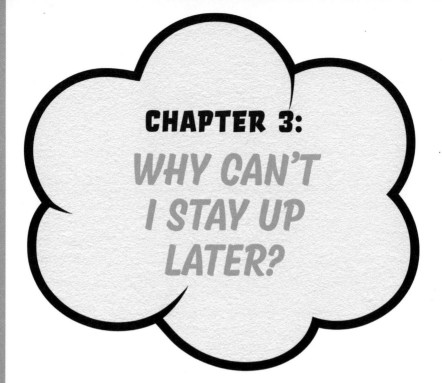

CHAPTER 3:

WHY CAN'T I STAY UP LATER?

sn't it unfair that your grown-ups (or older siblings) get to stay up later than you? It must be great not to have a "bedtime" and get to decide each night what time to go to bed. I'm sure you've had some late nights to remember—a big family event, a family trip, or even some nights when you've been sick. Those have been some pretty late nights! You might have felt tired the next day, or perhaps you got to sleep later the next morning, or even stay home from school.

Guess what?

When you were a tiny baby, you were up really late at night. A lot. You would be awake at 10 p.m. sometimes, or even at midnight. Or three o'clock in the morning! All babies are like that. Maybe you have a little sibling who is like that now. One reason they're up all night is because they need to eat all the time. But they also wake up a lot because their bodies haven't figured out how to get a good night's sleep. And besides, even with all of that late-night snacking and screaming, babies still sleep up to eighteen hours in a day! (And as you may know, one full day has only twenty-four hours). When they're very young, babies tend to do more daytime sleeping than night time sleeping.

But you're not a baby anymore. You're a big kid! So, why are your grown-ups so set on your bedtime? That's a great question. And the answer is not just because they want some quiet time without kids running around or because they do super awesome things while you're in bed. Have you ever left your room after bedtime to go to the bathroom and noticed what your grown-ups are doing? They're paying bills, doing dishes, folding laundry, and maybe even sleeping themselves, right? Totally NOT exciting stuff!

Sleep is really important. If you are ages 5 to 11 years old, you need about 9 to 11 hours of sleep each night. That's a lot! It's almost HALF of your day. Believe it or not, though, the (nearly) half of the day you are sleeping is just as important as the other half of the day when you're awake. Good sleep helps you:

- Grow
- Think
- Be smart
- Be strong
- Feel good
- Get sick less
- Not be crabby
- Do better in sports
- Be a better friend
- Make better food choices

Okay, you might say. Those all sound like pretty good things. Nobody wants to be in a bad mood, everyone wants to grow, do well in sports, and do well in school. Everyone wants to get along with friends, siblings, teachers, pets, grown-ups, and parents. But it's no fun to have to go to bed early. Sleeping is kind of like "doing nothing," so what's the point?

Well, there's a lot more to it, and, there are grown-ups out there who spend their entire days at work learning about and studying the science of sleep. Some are doctors who work in the field of "Sleep Medicine," and some are research scientists who study how the brain works during sleep. Many of these grown-ups spend their days trying to help other grown-ups and kids with sleep problems, because sleep is just as important for grown-ups as it is for kids. Grown-ups who have sleep problems also have trouble—difficulty at work, at home, and with their health and nutrition. It's no fun! But when their sleep is made better, these troubles get better, as well. Sleep is *definitely* more than just "doing nothing."

Let's go through a good night's sleep, to see what really happens.

When you first hit the pillow, sometimes you might fall asleep right away, but sometimes it might take some time. It's absolutely normal to stay awake for almost thirty minutes before you actually fall asleep. Maybe you're thinking about the day you just had, the day you'll have tomorrow, a fun event coming up, or even a test at school. Maybe you're thinking about a new toy you want, a great goal you scored at soccer, or even something not so pleasant—like a fight with a friend or a disagreement with your sibling. Or maybe you're just thinking that you can't fall asleep! All of these thoughts are normal and actually healthy. And when you do fall asleep, that's when the action begins.

There are five stages of sleep organized into what's called a **SLEEP CYCLE**. A sleep cycle lasts about two hours. Ideally, you want to have about FIVE cycles each night: 2 hours x 5 cycles = 10 hours. Each cycle begins with light sleep (stage 1), followed by deeper and deeper sleep (stages 2, 3, and 4). And then the deepest stage of sleep is **REM** sleep.

REM stands for **RAPID EYE MOVEMENT**. That's right, during your deepest stage of sleep, when your eyes are closed, your eyeballs move back and forth very quickly, as if you're looking right and left really fast. It's so fast that you can't even do it when you're awake. REM sleep is when you dream. Even if you wake up most mornings and can't remember a dream, or remember having had one but can't describe what it was about, you do dream during REM sleep. You dream five times each night! That's almost 2,000 dreams each year! By the time you go off to college, you'll have about 36,000 dreams! Those are some big numbers.

And why are dreams so important? Oddly enough, many scientists still don't know the exact reason why we dream. But many think it's a way for your brain to think about stuff that you wouldn't think about when you're awake. Maybe you've had adventure dreams, or scary dreams, or really, really strange dreams. Maybe you've had dreams that felt so real, you actually thought they WERE real. Whatever the dreams are about, it's your brain's way of "thinking" in a completely different way—one idea that scientists have is that dreams help you "clear your mind" for the next day, or help you work things out that might not have made sense to you before. Dreams take place during your deepest sleep, so even though some dreams may make you feel exhausted, they are actually the most restful part of your night.

Okay—so you know your brain does some important resting and free-thinking during sleep. What else is so important about it? Great question. Besides doing all that thinking, your brain does some other pretty amazing stuff, and a lot of it is when you sleep. Have you ever heard that someone has had a growth spurt? Or has anyone ever said to you, "Hey, did you grow over night?"

Kids grow at all different rates, and there is no right way or wrong way to grow. But a lot of your growing does depend on your sleep. A substance in your body actually helps make you grow—it's called **GROWTH HORMONE**. It's part of everyone's body, and it hangs out in your brain. When your body makes more of it, you grow. Growth hormone works extra hard during sleep. So, kids who don't sleep enough sometimes don't have enough growth **HORMONE**, and they may not grow as well.

On the other side, kids (and grown-ups) who don't get enough sleep may have more "hunger hormones" that get a bit out of control during the day. These hunger hormones go into overdrive if you're not sleeping enough, making you feel hungrier than you normally would, and perhaps making some not-so-healthy choices to eat. When you're tired from lack of sleep, you may want to eat to keep awake without even realizing it. And while having a sweet snack or juice or soda may give you a short burst of energy, you'll end up feeling just as tired, and even hungrier, as the day goes on. It's a sleepy hungry feeling!

Okay—you dream, you grow, and you eat well, all because of good sleep. What else?

Sleep affects your whole body—including your heart, your lungs, and even your **IMMUNE SYSTEM** (the infection- and cold-fighting part of your body). When you feel tired, your whole body feels tired. When you sleep, different parts of your body sleep in different ways. Let's start with an organ just as important as your brain: your heart.

When you're awake, say reading this or sitting at school, your heart beats about 75 to 90 times each minute—a little more than one time each second. Some other big numbers: Your heart beats 75 times per minute x 60 minutes x 24 hours = 108,000 heartbeats in just one day! That's about 39,420,000 times in just one year! Whew! When you're running around, your heart can beat 100 or more times per minute! That busy heart needs a rest! Thankfully, you have sleep. During your sleep, your heartbeat slows down to about 70 beats per minute. That gives it a chance to recharge for your busy day ahead.

And the same goes for your breathing—when you're reading this book, or sitting in class, you breathe about 20 times each minute. Some more numbers! That's about 20 times per minute x 60 minutes x 24 hours = 28,800 breaths in just one day! Or 10,512,000 breaths in just one year! Give those lungs a rest! When you're sleeping, you breathe about 12 times per minute. That helps give you energy to run around—you breathe up to 25 to 30 times per minute during recess or sports.

All of the good rest your brain, heart, and lungs are getting helps other parts of your body, too. Not getting enough sleep can make you more likely to get nasty colds, coughs, and sore throats. It can also make you be moodier—you may get in more arguments with friends and siblings, or you may not be able to pay attention as well at school. You may not perform at your best during sports. You may not be *feeling* tired, but your moodiness may be because of lack of good sleep. You may not be able to learn new things as quickly, or do as well on quizzes, tests, or projects. Many people have found that staying up late to cram for tests or finish projects do you no good the next day, and actually can do some harm. An extra hour of sleep is more valuable than an extra hour of studying. Your brain will work better the next day, and that extra hour of sleep will help you remember what you know better than an hour of cramming.

Hopefully I've convinced you that a regular, early bedtime is good for you! Sleep is like the best power food, coaching session, and even study session you can get.

If you have trouble keeping a good sleep schedule, here are some tips for you and your grown-ups:

TIP 1! Keep a regular bedtime, even on the weekends. You can stay up a little later when there's no school but not more than an extra half hour. Also (and here's the harder part), don't sleep much later during the weekend mornings. Ask your grown-up to wake you up or set an alarm clock. Believe it or not, there's no such thing as catching up on sleep.

TIP 2! Turn off any screens at least (AT LEAST!) one hour before bedtime. This includes iPads, TV's, laptops, phones, and video games. If you have your own electronics, ask your grown-up to store them and charge them  outside of your room at night. Maybe you can help them set up a charging station where all of the family's screens rest for the night! More on this in the chapter "Why Can't I Have More Screen Time?" (page 85).

TIP 3! The kitchen is closed one hour before bedtime. You can have a snack after dinner but not right before bed. No milk and cookies right before bedtime!

TIP 4! Start your bedtime routine about twenty minutes before your bedtime—wash face and hands, brush teeth, floss.

TIP 5! Reading a book, or having a book read to you, is an absolute, hands down, amazing, fantastic way to get ready for sleep.

TIP 6! Lights out! Sleeping in the darkness is the best way to sleep. If you can't sleep in the dark, a nightlight or dim light on in the hallway is a great option, but have a goal to saying good-bye to these at some point when you're ready.

TIP 7! Good night, sleep tight!

TIP 8! If you're not feeling well the next morning, check out the next chapter!

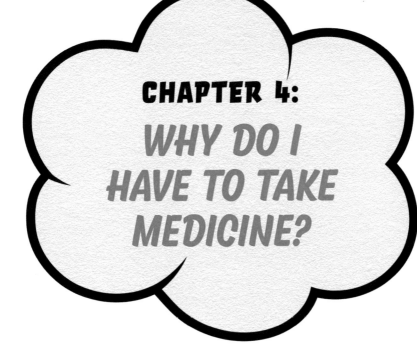

CHAPTER 4:

WHY DO I HAVE TO TAKE MEDICINE?

Some kids need to take medicine every day, or even a few times every day. If you're one of those kids, you may have had a hard time at first, but as you got used to it, I bet it got easier. Maybe your medicine is a liquid you drink, maybe it's a pill, maybe it's something you take as a breathing treatment, or maybe it's a shot. Maybe it's a type of sticker that sticks on your skin like a little piece of tape and delivers your medicine slowly all day. Maybe it's an ear drop, an eye drop, a skin cream, or a nose spray.

It's pretty amazing how many ways medicines can be given! Some kids with a condition called **DIABETES** have special pumps that sit under their skin that work throughout the day and night, giving medicine to help balance the levels of **GLUCOSE**, a type of sugar in everyone's bloodstream.

Whether you're a kid who takes medicine every day, or once per week, or almost never, sometimes when you're not feeling well, you may need to take medicine to help you feel better. That medicine is usually a liquid or a chewable tablet. Very rarely, it's given in the form of something called a **SUPPOSITORY**, meaning it's a tiny tablet that is placed very gently in your bottom. Usually, this method is only used if you're really having a hard time keeping down liquids from vomiting but need to get medicine into your body to make you feel better. There are thousands and thousands of medicines out there, but here we'll just talk about the really common ones that kids take when they feel sick, how they work, and what you can do to make them easier to take.

Kids of all ages sometimes get **FEVERS**. A fever is when your body temperature

gets really hot. Like really hot to the point that you feel kind of crummy—tired, achy, weak, or sore. Our body temperature typically ranges from 97°F to 99°F. If your temperature is roughly in that range, it's considered normal. But even a few degrees higher, say up to 101°F or 102°F, makes most people feel pretty bad. It's not the kind of hot you feel after running around on a warm summer day, where your cheeks might get flushed or you even sweat a bit. It's more of a feeling inside your body. A fever is often a sign that you have some sort of infection, either a cold or a cough, a sore throat, an ear infection, or even a flu or stomach virus. Having a fever is your body's way of reacting to something that's not quite right. Sometimes your doctor may recommend to treat your fever with rest, drinking lots of fluids, and not going to school or out to play. But sometimes your doctor will recommend taking a medicine to bring down your fever. That medicine won't get rid of your infection, but not having a fever will make you feel better.

When you have an infection, your body reacts by releasing certain substances that raise your temperature. The rise in your temperature may help kill off some of the causes of your infections (usually a

BACTERIUM or a **VIRUS**). But again, you'll be feeling kind of bad from the fever, so bringing it down to normal with a fever reducing-medicine is a great option.

SUPER IMPORTANT:

Take medicine ONLY if your most trusted grown-up is giving it to you. Sometimes this may be your school nurse, but only if your most trusted grown-up gave them permission to give you medicine. NEVER take it without them, and NEVER take any medicines (even vitamins) given by your friend's grown-up or from someone you don't know. EVER!

Okay, back to fevers: When you have a fever, sometimes you can feel really, really hot and even sweat. And then at other times, you can feel freezing cold, and even shake with chills. These are all normal actions that your body is taking to adjust to a temperature change of even a few degrees. It's really important to drink some extra fluids when you have a fever, since your body is releasing more fluid than usual just by sweating, having chills, or having a higher temperature.

A really common medicine given to reduce fevers for people of all ages, even babies, is something called **ACETAMINOPHEN**, commonly known as **TYLENOL.** This medicine can be given as a liquid, a chewable, a pill to swallow, or a suppository. It works by blocking one of the substances in your body that is signaling your temperature to rise. Another really common medicine for fever is called **IBUPROFEN**, also known as **MOTRIN** or **ADVIL.** This medicine also works by blocking substances in your body that cause fever and pain. You can take it as a liquid, as a chewable tablet, or a pill to swallow if you've learned how to do that. It's really important, however you take these, that you take the amount that your grown-up helping you tells you to, and that you take it as often as they recommend—not more and not less.

The other really common type of medicine that kids might need to take are a group of medicines called **ANTI-BIOTICS**. These are given to your grown-up by a doctor, meaning the doctor has to **PRESCRIBE** these. They are only given for very special instances and are to be taken only when your doctor recommends them. Antibiotics are given when you have an infection caused by a **BACTERIUM**. The funny thing (well, I think it's kind of funny!) is that we have millions (yes, many millions!) of bacteria living on our bodies all the time. Most of these bacteria are supposed to be there—helping our insides and outsides stay healthy and actually preventing us from getting sick. But a bad bacterium is a tiny organism that can set up shop in your throat, your nose, your digestive tract, your skin, or really just about anywhere it's not supposed to be. It can be very happy living where it shouldn't be and can make you feel pretty sick. Maybe you've had some sicknesses like ear infections, strep throat, skin infections, or even stomach infections caused by bacteria. Or maybe you haven't! But if you have, you may have taken something called antibiotics. These are medicines that help get rid of bacteria that shouldn't be there.

If you have an infection that's caused by a **VIRUS**, rather than bacteria, then you don't need to take antibiotics. You may feel the same way as you'd feel if your infection is caused by a bacteria (fever, sore throat, cough, stuffy nose, or stomach issues), but your doctor will just recommend rest, keeping your fever down if it makes you feel better, and drinking fluids if you can. Antibiotics won't work against viruses. Viruses enter cells and grow in the cells they invade and are REALLY good at "hiding" from antibiotics. Bacteria, on the other hand, are perfect targets for antibiotics, which are able to block the bacteria from growing.

Lots of kids who take any medicine, whether it's for a fever or an antibiotic, HATE it. (Here's a fun fact: your grown-ups don't like giving you medicine, either! Sometimes getting you to take your medicine may seem worse, to them, than the sickness itself!) There are lots of reasons kids don't like medicine. The biggies are: the taste (it tastes bitter, spicy, or just plain old yucky), the texture (it's too thick, too chalky, too grainy, or too slimy), the smell (it smells gross!), or the amount (it would be fine if you had to take just a drop or two, but one or two or even three teaspoons?? No way!). I wish I could give you the magic "poof" answer to making this easier. But there are some methods to try that will make the medicine go down much more easily.

METHOD 1 "Just a spoonful of sugar helps the medicine go down . . ." If you haven't seen the movie *Mary Poppins*, I highly recommend it! In it, Mary, a woman caring for two young children, sings a song about how to make medicine taste better. It's pretty simple! A spoonful of sugar! I know, I know—this is a book about not having cookies for dinner, not eating too much sugar because it can give you short but not long energy boosts and can also lead to some other health problems. But you're feeling sick! And that medicine tastes just awful, so a spoonful (or even half a spoonful) of sugar (or honey or agave or chocolate syrup or ice cream or grape jelly or sorbet or . . . you get the point, right?) makes a huge difference. It's pretty simple: Have your medicine ready on one (or two or however many) teaspoons, prepared by the trusted adult taking care of you, and the sweet stuff ready on another spoon. Take them one right after the other (medicine first!) and the taste will be so much easier to take! Some older kids like to change this up to a few small candy pieces (three m&m's are a great option), a few chocolate chips, a square of a chocolate bar, etc. Don't go too wild on the sweet stuff—it may upset your stomach, especially if you need to take your medicine three or four times per day for a few weeks. Some medicines NEED to be taken with a little food in your stomach, so you may even get a bit of a treat right before. This is because some medicines can irritate the inside lining of your stomach if there isn't a layer of food coating the stomach's lining. On occasion, a medicine may need to be taken on an EMPTY stomach. No food, no sweet treat, either before or during. Thankfully, this is really uncommon. But if your medicine needs to be taken this way, maybe you and your grown-up can decide on a fun treat you can have as soon as it's okay to do so, depending on the medicine's label and instructions. When in doubt, your grown-up can check with your doctor on this one.*

METHOD 2 Ice it! Here's a cool trick I've heard can do wonders: Chew some ice chips, suck on an ice cube, or even rub an ice cube on your tongue for about 10 to 20 seconds. It will numb your taste buds for a minute or two, so take the medicine right after this icy maneuver, and it should work great!

METHOD 3 Hold your nose! Sometimes the smell of medicine is worse than the taste. Squeeze your nose closed, and that will help you not only NOT smell it, but it will also block the bad taste as well.

METHOD 4 Psyche yourself up! Sometimes giving yourself a pep talk can help: "This is hard but I

---

* Fun fact! The man who wrote the song "A Spoonful of Sugar" for the movie Mary Poppins was inspired by his son, who received a sugar cube with a drop of medicine at school. That medicine was actually a polio vaccine, which used to be given as a drop of liquid taken by mouth, way back in the 1960s. The song writer, Robert Sherman, thought that giving medicine on a sugar cube was such a neat idea that he actually wrote a song about it!

can do it! I can do a lot of hard things, and this is one of them!" "If I take my medicine, I can get back to all the fun stuff I want to do!" "I used to fight back when my grown-up gave me medicine but now, I'm older and braver! I know I'm taking it to help me, so I can do this!"

Very few kids (or adults) *like* to take medicine but knowing that it's helping you get better can make a big, big difference in how you take it. A few "taste" tips can also make it easier for you to get it down. Another option is, if you're comfortable, and if the medicine is available, to learn how to swallow a pill. Many medicines come in pill form, and swallowing the pill avoids all the yucky taste issues. Sometimes learning to swallow a pill will take some practice. Some good tricks for pill swallowing include:

- Ask your grown-up to put the pill in something soft to eat that doesn't require much chewing, like a bit of nut butter, cheese, or soft bread. Eat the food as you normally would, "forgetting" that the pill is there, and down it goes!
- After you've gotten that down, the next step is to learn to swallow a pill with a sip of water.

- Drink a few sips of water first to get your body into "swallowing mode" as well as to moisten the back of your throat
- Place the pill toward the back of your tongue—not too far back where it would make you gag, but far enough so you can't really feel it sitting there.
- As you drink the liquid (water really is best for this), just concentrate on drinking and forget about the pill being there. It will slide right down!
- Remember, even big pills are much smaller than big chunks of food you swallow, even after chewing!

✳

Speaking of medicines of all shapes, consistencies, sizes, and types, sometimes when you go to a check-up appointment with your doctor, you need to get type of medicine in a shot. While many kids don't like taking medicine at home, many many MANY kids don't like getting a shot. It hurts! But read on to find out what they do, how they work, and why they are so important. And there are ways you can make them hurt less or not at all. (Really! Would I joke about this? Of course not!)

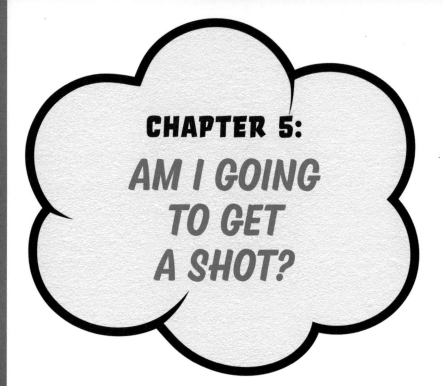

CHAPTER 5:

AM I GOING TO GET A SHOT?

Y ou've been to a lot of doctor's visits. Even if you're really healthy, you've gone to the doctor more times than you know! When you were a baby, you probably went *at least* every two months! And guess what? You got *at least* one shot at every visit until you turned one year old! After that, you probably only went for check-ups once or twice per year, and the other doctor visits were for if you were sick, had an injury, or if you have another issue that needs to be attended to by your doctor or a doctor who focuses on a specific area.

But once you were old enough to talk, usually some-time between ages one and two years, you probably

made it loud and clear, with that all-powerful word "No!" that you did NOT want a shot. Maybe you tried to squirm away from your grown-up's arms. Maybe you were quick enough to jump off of the doctor's table and run out of the room, hide in the waiting room, thinking that maybe they would change their minds and not give you that shot. I also bet that it never really worked. And I bet that you thought (and maybe still think!) that shots are a punishment! Because shots hurt! Why would a grown-up do something to you that hurts? Sometimes the shot hurts while you get it and it also hurts the next day, like someone punched you in your arm, your leg, or even your bottom! Maybe you feel yucky after shots, with a fever, aches all over your body, or even itchy with a rash in the area where you got the shot or even all around your body. Wow, this does sound awful. Why would grown-ups want to do this to you? Are they really that mean? And why can't shots be given like your other medicine, like a liquid you drink or a pill?

Now that you're older, and can talk more than you could when you were one or two years old, I'd bet you still feel pretty terrible about getting shots. Well guess what? Adults don't really like getting them, either! They hurt whether you're 2 months, 2 years, or 82 years old! The difference is, as adults we start to understand the importance of shots, how they help us, and how a tiny second or two of pain is much, much better than getting the illnesses that the shots are preventing.

A shot is sometimes called a **VACCINE.** A vaccine is a substance given to prevent a disease, not to treat it. They've been around for close to five hundred years, and each year, they get more and more perfected and more and more safe. They are given to prevent infections from viruses and bacteria. A vaccine is usually made of either parts of a virus, parts of a bacterium, or a dead virus or bacteria. When you receive a vaccine, certain cells in your body attach to certain parts of a virus or bacteria and create something called **ANTIBODIES**. These antibodies will protect you in the future if you get exposed to that particular virus or bacteria. Antibodies are like really powerful security guards, protecting you from evil intruders. Vaccines can be given as a shot, a liquid to drink, or as a nose spray, but most are still given as a shot.

Wouldn't it be great if shots didn't hurt? It sure would make those doctor visits a lot more pleasant! Shots do hurt—there's no doubt about it. They hurt for a few reasons. First, as you probably know, the material in the vaccine needs to get under your skin so it can get to your bloodstream and around your body. So, the material needs to get there through a tiny needle. The needle on a shot is not like a sewing needle or the point of a safety pin. The needle is actually thinner than a sewing needle or a safety pin, and it's hollow. The inside hollow part of the needle is where the fluid of the shot goes, from the **SYRINGE** (the plastic tube holding the shot material) into your body. These needles are super tiny—the tube in the hollow part is about 1/100th of an inch in diameter!

So why does such a tiny needle hurt so much? It's not much thicker than one of your hairs! And you certainly get more bumps and bruises every day, just being an active kid. What really hurts when you get a shot is the material in the liquid. No, it's not the virus particles or bacterial particles that hurt, but the liquid they are floating in. Sometimes that liquid is a bit thick, almost like oil. The reason it's thick is to help get the material to the right place in your body at the right speed. Liquid that's thicker sometimes hurts a bit more—it goes in more slowly and can sit for a longer time right under your skin where the shot was given.

This discomfort or pain can last a day or two after you get a shot. Usually it feels like a bruise, or like someone gave you a hefty punch in the arm. Sometimes you'll even feel a little bump or see some redness where you got the shot. This is usually a sign that your body, not just your sore arm, is starting to build those antibodies, or security guards, against the virus or bacteria.

Shots are given in areas with a bit of a cushion, like your upper arm or sometimes your thigh or your bottom. Some shots need to get into a bit of muscle, and the muscles of your arms and legs are usually pretty big and right under your skin. If you are concerned about being sore the next day, and you have a lot of writing to do or a sports game to play, ask your shot giver to give it in

your **NONDOMINANT** limb (the arm you don't write with, throw with, or kick with if it's your leg).

Vaccines work by tricking your body into thinking that it has to respond to something similar to an infection. But you actually don't have that infection! Not even a little bit! Many people think that getting a shot can cause the illness it's preventing. This is not the case. Your body develops protection by building up protective barriers, or blockers, kind of like really good goalies or security guards, against future infections. Sometimes if you feel not-so-great the day or two after a shot, it's because your body is working extra hard to build up those blockers. That can take a lot of work on the part of your protector cells, and it can, on occasion, make you feel tired, achy, or even feverish.

Shots are no longer made of the actual virus or bacteria. Instead, certain parts of these critters are used to create vaccines. Substances in your **IMMUNE SYSTEM** called antibodies go into action as they sense these pieces of virus or bacteria. The antibodies cling to the pieces, just like two perfectly matched pieces of a jigsaw puzzle. Once the antibodies make those connections, they are ready to stick to the real deal virus or bacteria in the future. When the puzzle pieces come together, the virus or bacteria can no longer live in your body. Your antibodies prevent that. Go, you!

Okay, but let's get back to the issue at hand. Shots hurt! And you don't want them! (I don't blame you, but hopefully you now know a little bit about how important they are to make your body strong enough to fight against some really nasty diseases out there). There are a few things you can do to help make shots hurt less. A lot less! Here you go:

5 MINDTRICKS TO MAKE A SHOT HURT LESS

1. Ask someone to watch as you're getting the shot. Right before the shot, have that person pinch your opposite arm or leg. It will be a startling distraction, and it really helps with minimizing the pain of the shot!

2. Some doctors' offices have a cooling spray to use. It works to "freeze" your skin for a few seconds and eases the sting of the needle poke.

3. There are products you can buy that have a mixture of vibration and coolness. This helps with preventing a shot from hurting, as well as helping with any soreness right afterward. Usually these are placed on your arm (or leg, or wherever the shot will be given) a minute or so before you get a shot.

4. Any distraction really helps. If you have a screen, pop up a funny video or your favorite song.

5. If you're feeling super brave, just think about how this tiny poke is preventing you from getting super sick. Sometimes just knowing that you are getting a bit of a superpower eases the pain of the poke.

Okay, you may say, it all sounds fine and good. How about shots for everyone else, but I'll skip them, thank you very much! Well, a cool thing about vaccines is that they protect not only the person getting them but also those around them. In fact, the only way that shots really work is if the majority (usually at least 90% or 95%, which means 90 or 95 people out of 100 people) of the population receives them. Otherwise, when an infection hits a community, many will remain unprotected, get sick, and spread it around.

If a very large percentage of a community is protected with a vaccine, the community develops something called **"HERD" IMMUNITY**, also known as community immunity. We are, after all, animals who live in herds, which include our homes, our neighborhoods, our schools, our cities, our countries, and our planet. Herd immunity is a way that a society that's vaccinated can better protect the very few people (around 5%) who *can't* get the shot because they are either too sick themselves, have severe allergies to the shots, or are receiving other types of medicines that make it unsafe for them to receive the shots. So, when you get your shots, you are not only protecting yourself, but you are also protecting your herd. Go, you!

These days, vaccines are subject to intense laboratory testing before any type of testing in humans is even considered. **IMMUNOLOGISTS**, who are doctors and researchers who study the immune system, are the experts who study, develop, and test new vaccines. They also fine-tune the ones that have been around for years, always retesting their safety, how well they work, who needs them, and how much each person needs.

✳

Whew! All this talk about shots has been stressful! If you're stressed from shots, or really from just about anything, you are not alone! What's the best way to tackle stress? Read on to find out!

CHAPTER 6:

WHY AM I SO STRESSED?

Do you get worried about things sometimes? Like whether you'll get your favorite teacher for your new school year? Or whether your team will win the baseball game? Or whether you goofed on that word you really thought you had down pat on your spelling test?

Everyone worries about things sometimes. It means we care! Sometimes worrying is a way of thinking through difficult situations, working out in your head what may or may not happen with all the possibilities ahead. If you don't get your favorite teacher, will you still be happy with the one you got? If your team loses the baseball game, will you all fall apart, or rally to support each other? If you missed that spelling word, I bet you'll never forget how to spell it again! Maybe you signed up for too many activities, and also got the hardest teacher, some extra chores to do around the house, and feel just so overwhelmed that you feel like you can't do anything at all! There are ways to cope with all of this, which we'll talk about in a bit.

But sometimes people (kids *and* adults) worry all the time, not necessarily about anything in particular, but just feel overall worried. Some grown-ups would call this being **ANXIOUS** or having **ANXIETY**. These are really common but really uncomfortable ways to feel, especially if the person feeling that way can't quite figure out what's giving them that feeling. Sometimes it's called **STRESS**, which is more of a feeling of being overwhelmed with thoughts about what's going on.

These are all very important issues to think about and to talk about with a trusted adult—a parent, a relative you trust, a coach, a counselor, or a teacher. Sometimes one of these folks can help you work through these tough feelings. But sometimes, you might need a little more help, and that's okay, too. You may want to speak with a psychologist—an adult who works with kids who have a lot of stress, worry, or anxiety. My best advice to you is to never worry alone! It really does help to share your worry with someone you trust.

Imagine carrying two huge bulky bags of groceries up a steep flight of stairs. Some of the groceries topple out of the bags with each step you take, setting you back even more. Wouldn't it be easier if someone else held one of those bags? The groceries would still be carried, but it would be a group effort! And much easier. And imagine if not only someone helped you, but they also added handles to the bags, so they weren't so bulky and hard to manage! Easier even still.

Being stressed and anxious is like carrying those heavy bags up those steep steps by yourself: when you try to hold it all on your own, it makes it even harder. There are always people around you who are there to help—even those you may not think of as helpers. And you never know, one day *you* may be the one to help a friend or family member with something that's making them stressed or worried!

Even with helpers, it's really common (and very normal!) to worry. Sometimes worrying about something makes it hard to sleep, hard to focus at school, hard to enjoy playing with friends or playing sports or music, and even hard to enjoy a favorite food. Sometimes what's worrying you takes up all of your energy, and you can't think about anything else, can't do anything else, and certainly can't enjoy anything else.

There are a lot of things you can do on your own, even without your helpers, that can help with your worrying. What I like to do is really think about what's making me stressed or worried, and what parts of that I can take control over.

Okay, let's think of an example: The try-outs for the school play are this week, and you've been practicing lines and songs for the part you really want. You've seen the play performed by adults, know the lines like the back of your hand, and think you'd be perfect for the part. Turns out, a few of your good friends have the exact same idea about themselves—they know the lines and songs, have seen the play a zillion times, and think that *they'd* be perfect for the part. That's probably one of the reasons why you're all friends—you have similar interests!

Well, the reality is that one of you will get the part. It might be you, but it might not. And not getting this part may seem like the worst possible thing in the world. So besides preparing for the try-out, how do you ease your stress?

One way to handle this is to play out the possibilities in your head, with you getting the part and with one of your friends getting the part. Try to imagine how each will feel. In addition, see how your friends will feel if it's you who gets it. In one option, you'll probably feel great, and in the other, not so much.

Well, guess what?

It is perfectly okay to feel really sad, really disappointed, and even a bit angry if it's not you who gets the part. You may even shed some tears. That's also okay! Emotions can be big, can be overwhelming, and may even catch you by surprise. You may find it hard to congratulate your friend on something they got that you wanted so much. That's really hard. Maybe you'll tell them the next day, or that night you can text them or call them to congratulate them.

Lots of kids (and adults!) are worried about how they will feel if something doesn't go their way, but feelings that are sad or angry are just as normal as feelings that are happy and joyful. It's not okay to display anger where you'd hit another person, throw things, or use unkind language, but feeling bad or sad are parts of life. And believe it or not, these disappointments and bad feelings make it easier to handle tough situations as you get older. A skill that's really hard, but really important, to master is called **EMPATHY**. This is where you "put yourself in someone else's shoes." Well, not *really* into their shoes, just pretending! Empathy is recognizing and appreciating the feelings of others—whether they are happy, sad, angry, or disappointed.

What if you're just stressed about "everything"? You're worried, overwhelmed, and feel nervous, but can't really pinpoint what it is? There's no school play to audition for, no big spelling test or project, and no big family event coming up. You're just stressed! This is also really common (and really normal!). We live in a pretty complicated world, and a lot is going on during your day that might make you stressed. When you're feeling this way, one thing you can do is picture a typical day (usually a school day), and go through, in your mind, each part of your day. Really picture it—what you're doing, who you're with, and, most important, how it makes you feel when you picture it. As you do this, you might think *Bingo!* "I get really upset when Katie sits in the seat I want on the bus!" or "Dad always makes my toast too crunchy!" or "I'm really having a hard time with division and subtraction!"

If nothing comes to mind, though, go back to our first plan—talk to someone! A parent, a sibling, a friend, a teacher, a coach, a counselor, or someone you like and trust. Sometimes all you need to say is "I feel really stressed," and the conversation will go from there. I bet they'll start talking about what's stressing them out, too!

Another really important technique to help with your stress is (you may not want to hear this) to cut back your use of technology. You know—computers, phones, television, video games, and really anything that's on a screen. When you're watching or playing, your brain works in ways that it doesn't when you're reading a book, talking to a friend, or running around. And the way your brain is working when you're on a screen can increase your stress levels, even hours after you've turned off the screen. Believe me, I know it's hard to do, but reducing screen time will really help with reducing your stress. Try it!

Other ways to help with stress, whether it's stress from something specific or stress from just, well, everything, include helping your body relax. If your body relaxes, often your brain will follow. Some kids like to do yoga, stretching, or breathing exercises. Some kids have learned to meditate.

TRY THIS! ACTIVITY

Sometimes it's as simple as trying a simple breathing exercise. Here's one that some kids like to do. It's called 4-7-8, and you can do it anywhere, anytime! It's super simple, and you can do it during a stressful time, like right before a test or a performance, or just on your own if you're feeling stressed. Here goes:

Breathe in through your nose (okay, if you have a cold and are super stuffy, breathe in through your mouth), and as you do this, count to four. Slowly.

1 . . . 2 . . . 3 . . . 4.

When you've filled up your lungs, HOLD that breath in and count silently to seven. Again, really slowly.

1...2...3...4...5...6...7.

Then, breathe out really really slowly, and count silently to eight.

1...2...3...4...5...6...7...8.

Repeat!

This exercise will relax your breathing, your heartbeat, and will distract you from what you're stressed about because you'll be focused on your breathing. It can really help, and you don't need to be in a yoga pose or in a special meditation time to do it. It literally can be done anywhere, anytime. And for as long as you'd like!

And some kids are thinking, "No way! I'm not doing any of that!" That's fine, too. There's no "right" way to relieve stress. But it's really important for you to find a few techniques that might work for you. Maybe you picture yourself on your favorite vacation, playing your favorite sport, listening to your favorite music, or reading a favorite book. You may be able to actually listen to that music or read that book if you have them around. Some kids have a favorite book they turn to, many years after they've read it a hundred times, but just thumbing through it makes them feel relaxed. It's a great technique! Or that favorite song, even if you're a fifth grader and loved it in kindergarten. The important thing is to recognize when you're feeling stressed. That could be the hardest part. And once you feel it, you'll have some great tools to handle it.

For many kids and grown-ups, stress is a regular part of life. Even every day! Many people find ways to handle stress that work best for them—a quiet time reading, taking a warm bath, talking to a friend or grown-up, regular breathing exercises, yoga or meditation. Whatever you find to relieve stress (and it can be more than one activity that works for you), it's good to make a habit of it. If you do your stress-relieving technique regularly, even when you're not feeling stressed, you may notice that you're not stressed as often!

※

And speaking of routines, we all know of certain routines that may not be as fun or relaxing as daily stress-relieving exercise, but they're just as important!

Pass the toothpaste, please!

CHAPTER 7:

DO I HAVE TO WASH MY HANDS AND BRUSH MY TEETH _AGAIN_?

Let's see if this sounds familiar—you're about to have dinner, and your grown-up asks, "Did you wash your hands?" You proudly say, "Yes!" And then comes "With soap??" You plod back to the sink. . . .

Why are grown-ups so set on soap? Isn't washing with water pretty good as a way to get clean? And you did it without being told! And that toothbrushing! It's such a drag. Yeah, the strawberry-bubblegum-cotton-candy-watermelon-fruity-lishous flavor is pretty good, but isn't once in the morning enough in the toothbrushing world? You have other things to do!

We'll start with the soap story, which seems to be a common request of many adults. Soap is what you think of as a bar of soap at the sink or shower or bathtub, laundry detergent, dishwashing liquid, or the liquid in a soap dispenser in a public restroom. Those are all soaps, but **SOAP** is actually a type of chemical compound. When scientists refer to "soap," they may mean something really specific, not the stuff you're supposed to wash your hands with. But the soap they're talking about is also the material that makes up the soap at the sink!

Soap is a type of **MOLECULE** made of fats and salts. It's a long, skinny molecule with many parts to it. One end of the molecule loves water, and one end loves oils and germs. When a bunch of soap **MOLECULES** get together, they form a circle, and it looks like a pretty flower or a bicycle wheel with a lot of spokes. The outer parts of the circle (like the flower petals or the outer part of the

bicycle wheel) love water, and the inner parts love oil and germs. These "soap flowers" are called **MICELLES.** The oil-loving centers of these soap flower micelles help dissolve dirt, grease, and germs. The water-loving part of the micelle attract water, so when you're washing your hands with soap, the soap gets foamy as it dissolves. Warm water (but not too hot!) helps melt or soften the oil and germy stuff, helping it stick to the oil-loving parts of the micelles. Major bonus if you rub the soap around on your hands for at least 20 seconds.

When you're finished washing with soap and rinsing with water, it's time to dry your hands. While some public restrooms have warm air dryers, giving that whoosh of air either after you push a button or when you run your hands near the dryer, drying with a clean paper towel is best. This is because, when you use the towel, the rubbing on your skin helps continue to clean it. It can scrape (without really scraping—you don't want to rub too hard!) any remaining dirt and germs off your skin. If you don't dry them, they can get dirty again pretty quickly, as people tend to use their pants, their friend's shirt, or the ground to dry them off!

Even though you may not have olive oil all over your hands (or face), other types of dirt and germs from playing, doing homework, or helping cook dinner need to come off by washing. With soap *and* water! Shampoo is just a form of soap and does the same cleaning

TRY THIS! ACTIVITY

If you want to see why it's so important for soap to have both water-loving and oil-loving parts, try rubbing a little bit of oil, like olive oil, on your hand. Now try washing it off with just plain cold water. Not so easy, right? Add a little soap to that cold water, and the oil-loving part of the soap will get to work and wash that oil right off! Now try a little oil on your skin, and add warm, soapy water. That should be the fastest, easiest, and most thorough way to get that job done!

job for your hair. You know you need both shampoo and water to get your hair clean. And just like the soap at the sink, it's always best to rinse it all away after you're finished scrubbing and cleaning. Leftover soap left on hands or hair gets very slimy! The best way to get rid of extra soap? Extra water!

Some very specific times it's really important to wash your hands (with soap) include:

- After you use the restroom
- Before and after you eat a meal or a snack
- After you play sports, inside or outside
- If you get dirty for any reason
- After you play with shared toys at school
- Before you go to a friend's house to play
- When you get home from a playdate

Can you think of any others?

You use soap to wash your hands, face, and body—and what is toothpaste if not soap for your mouth? (Except we know it's not really soap!) Your teeth (and your gums!) need your super attention, even before your grown-up choppers come in.

You may have lost a tooth or a bunch of teeth already, or maybe you still have all your baby teeth. But even those first ones, those baby teeth that fall out anyway, need some really good care. Yes, you'll get a second chance with your

grown-up teeth, but it's really important to take care of the first ones, too. In fact, even before you *had* teeth (check out a baby who's under age one year—they may have only a few teeth, or even none at all), it was pretty important to keep your gums clean and healthy. Your gums are the homes of your teeth, and who doesn't want a clean, healthy home for your pearly white choppers?

Think for a minute what hangs out on your teeth—some leftover food, some drinks, and, believe it or not, germs! Yes, germs live in your mouth. Most of them are good germs, actually "good **BACTERIA**," that help keep some of the not-so-good germs (bacteria) away. Some of the not-so-good bacteria like to set up homes, and grow their families, in your teeth. They love sugar and other bacteria, both of which help them grow and multiply.

When these bacteria have plenty of sugar, leftover foods, and sticky stuff left in your mouth, they can form tiny holes in your teeth known as **CAVITIES**. These cavities can hurt! And the dentist may have to put some material in those holes so they don't get bigger; this is called getting a "filling."

One way to prevent cavities and keep your teeth and gums healthy is to brush them! You probably already know that you're supposed to brush your teeth, because I'm sure more than once you've been told "Go brush your teeth!" Maybe you like to brush. Maybe you like your toothpaste, and maybe you like that clean feeling in your mouth afterward. Maybe you hate it! Or maybe you just feel like it's a big waste of time. You have better things to do! Well, however you feel, it's something that's really important for you and your health.

We just learned what's in soap and how washing your hands with it really works. What's in toothpaste? Well, you know that some toothpaste has some sort of flavoring—fruity, bubblegum, or mint. But the ingredients that make toothpaste clean your teeth are: anti-bacterial agents to get rid of those overgrowing bacteria, baking soda, and **FLUORIDE**. Most toothpastes contain other

ingredients, but these are the three most important to keep your teeth clean.

You may be wondering why baking soda (wait—wasn't that an ingredient in cookies?) would be in tooth-paste, as well.

If you have any baking soda at home, ask an adult if you can take a bit and put it in a bowl. First, notice how it feels. Not like soda, really. But not like flour or sugar. It's a little gritty, which is why it helps scrub teeth! It's also a little bit salty (although it tastes pretty yucky, fair warning) but also what's called **ALKALINE**. Something that's alkaline is also known as a **BASE**. This is a substance in chemistry that reacts with other substances called **ACIDS** to make salt or water. Lots of cleaning products in your home, like laundry detergent, are alkaline.

The opposite of alkaline is called **ACIDIC**. Examples of acidic substances are vinegar, lemons, fruit juices, and . . . the bacteria in your mouth! When you mix something acidic (like the bacteria in your mouth) and something alkaline (like baking soda), you can "even things out," or **NEUTRALIZE**, so it's more like water. Neutralizing is similar to setting something in balance. Say you and your friend are on a seesaw. You are the acid and your friend is the base. If the base is bigger, the seesaw will lean toward your friend. If the acid is bigger, the seesaw will lean more toward you. If you can both balance, by one of you scooting forward or backward in your seat, you can make the seesaw float, in balance. Neutral! Neither acid nor base.

TRY THIS! ACTIVITY

If you still have that baking soda handy, you can get some other ingredients and make homemade toothpaste! It probably won't taste as good as the kind you'd buy at the store, but you can see how simple it can be made. All you need is:

6 teaspoons of baking soda

1/3 teaspoon of salt

4 teaspoons of glycerin (also called "vegetable glycerin" and can be bought at the grocery store in the baking section)

15–20 drops of mint flavoring (or really any flavoring!)

Mix all the ingredients in a small bowl, store it in a container with a lid, and voila! Homemade toothpaste!

Okay, maybe you prefer the store-bought kind, but now you know it's pretty simple, and the main ingredient is baking soda, which acts as a scrubber as well as an alkaline to neutralize the acidic stuff (bacteria) on your teeth!

And here's what many kids really don't like, as it can seem to take up a lot of time, and it can be tricky to do: flossing! But flossing teeth is super important. When you brush, you clean the surface of your teeth, but not the spaces between your teeth. Food and bacteria absolutely love living between teeth, and the best way to get rid of them is to floss. Most kids have about 20 teeth before kindergarten, so flossing can feel like a big waste of time—times 20! And the string is sticky and tricky! The good thing is that there are now so many different types of flosses to use. Talk with your grown-up, or with your dentist, about the different types, and find one that works best for you. There's a floss for everyone out there! And once you get the hang of it, you'll see it really doesn't take up too much time.

As you may imagine, brushing your teeth helps scrub and alkalinize your teeth for a while, and flossing cleans out the spaces between the teeth, but doing them once won't last forever! Brushing should be done at least twice per day (or three times per day, if possible) and flossing at least once each day. Fluoride is added to most toothpastes to help prevent cavities and protect the coating of each tooth. This coating is called **ENAMEL**. If the enamel gets worn down, cavities can form. This is why you should brush your teeth when you wake up in the morning, after meals, and before bedtime. No need to scrub them too hard, and you only need a pea-sized amount of toothpaste each time. And don't forget to floss right after! Rinse your mouth with a little water afterward to remove any of the leftover toothpaste hanging around. You'll feel fresh and clean!

Having a clean mouth is a win! While you might not win any prizes for cleanest mouth of the year, you'll have great check-ups at your dentist and probably won't need to go to extra visits to get cavities filled. Some kids love going to the dentist because a lot of dentist offices now have movies playing, virtual reality goggles, and cool video games in the waiting room. That might sound like a win!

✳

Speaking of winning, movies, and video games, let's talk about screen time. . . .

CHAPTER 8:
WHY CAN'T I HAVE MORE SCREEN TIME?

We do love our screens. Many kids can work a keypad on a laptop or even a phone before they are potty trained! Maybe that was you. Or maybe you first tried screen games and watched shows when you started elementary school. Chances are, the adults and any older kids in your house use screens as much as, if not more than, you.

Screens can be beneficial in many ways. They provide access to learning, to playing, to being entertained, and to communication with friends, family, and teachers. Technology changes every day, and the ability to be creative and innovative has also grown as screens have become more advanced. Screens get a bad rap, but there's a lot of good to them. But . . . as much as it hurts to hear, there's also a lot of bad. Which is why it's really important to understand both sides of the screen story.

When we think about how a screen, or digital device, affects you, for good or for bad, let's start at the top. Your **BRAIN**! Your brain is more complex, creative, and flexible than any computer around. The most complicated brain codes can change in a flash. And unlike many screen games, with pre-set programming, the cells inside of your brain, known as **NEURONS**, are growing every day. These neurons are unique cells that live in your nervous system, which includes your brain, your **SPINAL CORD** (which is the messaging center, like an amazingly powerful telephone wire), and your **NERVES**.

The nerves are tiny fibers, like the thinnest telephone wires you can imagine, that signal your muscles to do things like walk, sit, stand, or move your eyes back and forth across a page. Your brain is the control center for all your nerves, and it is filled with those tiny cells called neurons. How many of those tiny cells, you might ask? Well, 86 BILLION of those tiny cells! Here's what that number looks like: 86,000,000,000! That's 86 plus nine zeros!

As you grow, those neurons become more and more mature and active. Especially in kids like you, who are learning and growing every day, those neurons are working hard. Each of your neurons contain material that helps send a message to the next neuron, which sends a message to the next one, and so on, and so on, and so on. It's really important at all stages of life, but especially when you're a kid, to strengthen those neurons, making your brain and nervous system ready to handle new things that you learn as the years go by. Too much screen time can prevent that growth from reaching its full potential.

Your nervous system is the most complex messaging system in the world! More than any smartphone app around. And it's more important, too. Yes, technology can be creative, and even smart, but it doesn't have the individual thoughts, ideas, feelings, and actions that a human has. This is why it's important to remember that, while technology is great, YOU are greater. Your family is greater. Your friends, your teachers, your coaches, and yes, your pets, are greater.

Let's first talk about some of the good stuff that happens with screens. Games that you can play can be really fun, clever, and even help you with hand-eye coordination, reflexes, thinking ahead, and being creative. All good! Some people even say surgeons can get better at certain types of surgery by playing video games! Screens also have great educational material, including websites to help with math skills, reading skills, and writing skills. Most books can now be read on a screen, and some books come with the option to read it as well as having someone read it aloud along with you. Some kids learn how to "code" on screens, where they can create their own games, projects, robots, and so much more. This can be creative and can lead to designing things that have never been done before. Pretty amazing!

Sometimes if you need to learn about something quickly, or have a burning desire to find the answer to a question, a screen, or even a "talking screen," can provide that for you. "What was the number one song of the third week of October in 1971?" You can find that out in less than a second. Cool!

When you're waiting around before dinner, you can click on a video and get a good laugh for a minute or two. And then click another video and get another laugh. And another. And another. And another. You may keep clicking and clicking until you soon forget that your family's calling you for dinner, or it's time for school, or time for bed. And that's one way that screens can turn not-so-good pretty quickly.

The power they have to pull us in (ALL of us) can be distracting, and we can easily lose track of what's going on in our world. Our REAL world. Notice I'm not saying "*you* can easily lose track" but "*we* can easily lose track"? This is because screens are just as good, and just as bad, for grown-ups as they are for kids. Grown-ups can get distracted just as much as, if not more, by screens, than kids can.

When we get wrapped up in screen time, it makes us lose our sense of time and even makes us forget how to treat one another. Some screen games have a lot of fighting, explosions, and destruction. While you probably know that it's all pretend, even when you're deep into one of these games, the makers of these games are clever enough to make you feel a certain way—like you're really fighting and really seeing explosions and destruction. Yes, you know it's a game, but the power of losing yourself in such a game makes it hard to step away and hard to get back to your real world. You may even start to feel that certain screen games *are* your real world. If that's the case, the game makers have succeeded.

You may also notice (well, you may not notice, but someone may point it out) that you get really grumpy and angry when your adult asks to you to stop playing on your screen. It may take them several asks. They may start giving warning times. Or start counting. Or take your screen out of your hands while you're in the middle of a very important battle on your game. If that happens, you might get really *really* grumpy, or really *really* angry. Your adult may get angry and grumpy, too.

Many screen games are designed to have no specific end, which makes it hard for anyone to win and/or finish the game. If this happens a lot in your house (it happens a lot in many houses), your grown-up may create some screen boundaries—either limiting the amount of time, limiting which days you can use a screen, or cutting out certain games altogether. Yes, this will feel like punishment, but it really is a way to help your brain get a break from all of the screen time.

Try picturing a little baby. The baby is being pushed in a stroller on a beautiful spring day in their neighborhood. While they're in the stroller, a bunch of kids in the neighborhood are playing ball, some are on their bikes, and some are playing tag. But the baby is holding a small screen and is thoroughly engaged in a cartoon. When the cartoon is finished, another one pops up. And then another one. The baby is missing the beautiful day, the flowers blooming with all of their different colors. The baby is missing the chance to watch the kids play, to see what riding a bicycle looks like. To hear bigger kids talk and laugh and figure out who's "it" and who's running.

Well, you're certainly not a baby, but this baby you've imagined is showing you that you can miss a lot when you're glued to your screen. It may not feel that way, since many kids (and yes, many adults) feel that they are missing out on something when they're *not* on their screen. But it really is the opposite.

Here's something to try (but only if your grown-up approves):

TRY THIS! ACTIVITY

Try watching a show or playing a game on a screen for ten minutes while you're out at a park, a beach, or sitting in a restaurant. It has to be exactly ten minutes and then you have to turn it off. Then try to describe what you saw at the park, the beach, or the restaurant. Try another ten minutes of being present in your environment and describe it again. You might say, "The screen was better! Nothing was going on!" But there was. I promise.

When you don't have your head down and your eyes on the screen, you can see people interact and animals flying, buzzing, or climbing. You feel the weather. The wind. The noises. It may feel like "nothing" because your brain has become used to tuning out all of the non-screen stuff. But it's all there, and just like that baby who's missed out on watching and learning, we all miss something when our eyes are on a screen.

You may hear the term "screen time" being thrown around, and you may feel that your amount of screen time is not enough. Part of the reason for this is that time seems to move differently when you're on a screen. If you have twenty minutes of screen time, and fifteen minutes go by and you get the "Five more minutes!!" warning, you may think, *There is no way I only have five more minutes! I just started!* Well, that same twenty minutes spent practicing piano might feel a lot different. This is again because we (yes, WE) can lose track of just about everything, including time, when we're on a screen. Maybe that's because we're having so much fun, but maybe, just maybe, it's because we lose a little track of the real world around us.

The MOST important time to turn off your screens is right before bedtime. Your getting-ready-for-bed time and your actual bedtime should include moments of winding down, settling down, relaxing, and getting into the quietest time of your day. It's not the time to get in that last battle, giggle at just one more silly video, or watch a show. Screen time in the hour before sleep time (and this goes for adults, too) messes up the good quality of sleep you need. So even if you get enough hours of sleep, being on a screen right before sleep can disrupt how deeply you sleep and how well you dream.

And there's more (there's always more!).

Even if your screen is OFF but is charging in your room, the light that's peeking through your screen, known as "blue light" (even if it doesn't look blue), can mess with your sleep quality. It's best to charge all screens in a different room from where you sleep. If that's not an option, try to have the screen and charger completely out of your view, such as under a chair or desk.

Okay, so screens are good. I said it! (You can quote me!) But that's not the end of the line, because there's a lot about them that's not so good. Most of the not-so-good is related to all of us—babies, kids, and adults—being unable to put them down when we've had enough. Or even more than enough.

Here are some tips (for you!) to help you manage your screen time:

TIP 1! Set your own timer! Try to do this yourself, and show your grown-up how it's done. It won't be easy! But if you can agree on an amount of time together and stick to it, you will save yourself a lot of anger and frustration later.

TIP 2! Play your favorite game and have someone else look at a timer. Have them pick a time to yell "Stop!" And you guess how long you think it was. This will give you an idea of your "sense of time" during your screen time. It may surprise you! (Nine minutes? It felt like nine seconds!)

TIP 3! Keep a log for one week of sleeping time when you're off a screen for at least one hour (yes, one hour!) before bedtime. See how you feel that week!

TIP 4! Ask your grown-up to try these tips, too.

SOME FINAL THOUGHTS FROM ME TO YOU!

Wow, thank you so much for spending some time reading this! Whether you read it on your own, read it to a younger sibling or friend, or read it with a grown-up, I truly hope that you now feel you can take on the world with your healthy self! I also really hope that these chapters sparked your interest in how your body works, in ways that you hadn't even thought of before, and, more importantly, how you can take control of your healthy self. A BIG reminder is that nobody (and nobody's body, of course) is perfect, or even close to perfect. So, if you try to be healthy but slip up, know that you are not alone! We all want to be healthy, strong, happy, and feel great, but we are also human! My advice to you is to keep asking questions, share what you know, and be open to new things. You never know what you might learn!

SUPER HEALTHY ME

Now it's your turn to share what "super healthy you" likes to do to stay healthy!
Feel free to jot down words, pictures, or both!

My favorite breakfast is: _____

_____

My favorite lunch is:

_____

My favorite snack is:

_____

My favorite dinner is:

_____

My favorite cookie is: _____

       It looks like:

I know how to cook/make: _____

_____

I want to learn how to cook/make: _____

_____

My favorite thing to do at recess is: _____

_____

My favorite sport is: _____

_____

Here's me playing my favorite sport:

_____

I would like to learn how to play: _____

_____

I always wear a helmet when I: _____

_____

My bedtime on school nights is _____,
and I wake up at _____ on
school days.
I get _____ hours of sleep on school nights.
My bedtime on weekends is _____, and I wake up at
_____ on weekends.
I get _____ hours of sleep on weekends.
My favorite bedtime book is _____
_____

My favorite dream was when: _____
_____
_____
_____
_____
_____

When I need medicine, I take (circle one):
       Liquid. Chewable. Pill. Other.

Here is how I will try to make it easier to take medicine:
_____
_____
_____
_____

I like getting a shot at the doctor's (circle one)
YES (wow!!)
NO (join the crowd)

Next time I need a shot, here's what I'll try to do to
make it easier: _____

_____

_____

When I get stressed, I react by: _____

_____

_____

Next time I get stressed, here's what I'll try: _____

_____

_____

_____

Here are some of my favorite helpers for when I'm
stressed: _____

_____

_____

Here's who I have helped (or will help) when they get
stressed: _____

_____

My favorite soap is: _____

Favorite soap? That was a silly question.

My favorite shampoo smell is: _____

_____

My favorite toothpaste flavor is: _____

_____

I brush my teeth _____ times each day.

I will try to brush my teeth _____ times each day.

I floss my teeth every day. (circle one)

YES (superstar)

NO, but I will try (superstar-in-training)

I counted my teeth. I have _____ teeth!

I have _____ baby teeth and _____ grown-up teeth.

(Fun fact, if you have your 6-year-molars or 12-year-molars, these are grown-up teeth that came in without baby teeth even falling out!)

I spend _____ minutes* on my screen each school day, not including screen use at school.

I spend _____ minutes on my screen each weekend day.

> You can show your work here;

*There are 60 minutes in each hour, so if you use a screen for more than one hour, multiply the number of hours by 60. If you haven't learned how to do this yet, ask an older person and they can show you.

Here's some quick math:

1 hour = 60 minutes

1½ hours = 90 minutes

2 hours = 120 minutes

2½ hours = 150 minutes

3 hours (ARE YOU ON YOUR SCREEN FOR THREE HOURS???) = 180 minutes

I will do _____ instead of screen time sometimes.

GLOSSARY

ABDOMINAL: Location in the front part of the body, from the lower rib cage area to just above the hips. Abdominal muscles are the muscles in that region.

ACETAMINOPHEN: Commonly known as Tylenol®, a medication used to help bring fevers down, and sometimes to help ease pain such as headaches or body aches.

ACIDIC/ACID: A substance with a lower pH than water, which has a pH of 7.0.

AEROBIC: When related to exercise, something that involves lots of movement, faster breathing (aerobic literally means 'oxygen-using'), and faster heart rate. Examples include running, swimming, and biking.

ALKALINE/BASE: A substance with a higher pH than water, which has a pH of 7.0.

AMINO ACID: A large molecule that is part of a much larger substance called a protein.

ANTIBIOTIC: A medication prescribed by a doctor to treat an infection caused by a bacteria.

ANTIBODIES: A type of protein produced by the body as a response to an infection, blocking the infecting substance from growing and spreading. Antibodies protect us from getting sick if we are exposed to a certain infection.

ANUS: The last area of the digestive system where feces (poop) exits.

ANXIETY: A condition with extreme nervousness and worry.

ANXIOUS: Experiencing worry or nervousness.

BACTERIUM/BACTERIA: A microscopic organism made of one cell that can act to help balance an internal area of the body, or can cause illness if either the bacteria multiplies too much, or if it's a harmful bacteria not meant to be in the body.

BALANCE: In physical activity, the ability to withstand something unstable, such as standing on one leg, riding a bike, or balancing on a beam.

BRAIN: The organ in the skull that contains over one billion cells called neurons, and acts as the 'command center' for the rest of the body.

CARBOHYDRATE: An energy-providing substance in foods, made of carbon, hydrogen, and oxygen atoms to make larger molecules such as sugar and starch. In foods such as pasta, bread, cookies, and rice.

CARBON: An element that commonly bonds to other elements to form larger compounds, especially carbohydrates or carbon dioxide (the gas we breathe out). In its simplest form, it can be found as graphite or diamonds.

CELL: The smallest unit of life, contained in all living things. It can divide and multiply on its own.

DEHYDRATED: Not having enough water to keep the body functioning well.

DIABETES: A condition where a person has trouble regulating the balance of sugar (glucose) in the bloodstream, often due to a lack of insulin from the pancreas. Diabetes is managed by carefully administering insulin under the close care of a doctor.

DIGESTION: The process of breaking down food after eating. Part is used for energy to the body, and the remainder is waste.

ELEMENT: A substance that is so small it cannot be broken down into smaller parts. Examples include carbon, hydrogen, oxygen, and calcium.

EMPATHY: Being able to know how someone else is feeling.

ENDURANCE: The ability to do something for a set amount of time.

ENZYMES: Substances in the digestive system that help break down larger particles in to smaller ones, enabling the smaller ones to provide nutrition and energy to the body.

ESOPHAGUS: The muscular tube that transports food from the mouth to the stomach.

FAT: A major fuel source for the body, contained in foods such as butter, nuts, meat, and dairy products such as milk and cheese.

FEVER: When the body temperature increases beyond the average body temperature to above 100.4°F (38°C).

FIBER: a substance in some foods which cannot be broken down by enzymes during digestion. It can help to slow digestion and can also help to remove wastes from the digestive tract.

FLEXIBIITY: In physical activity, the ability to bend joints comfortably.

FLUORIDE: An element that is found in toothpaste (and most tap water supplies) which helps reduce tooth decay.

GLUCOSE: The simplest carbohydrate, also known as sugar, which contains carbon, hydrogen, and oxygen.

GROWTH HORMONE: A substance produced in the brain that signals other parts of the body (bones, muscles, etc.) to grow.

HERD IMMUNITY: The concept that if enough people in a certain population are immune (by vaccination) to an illness, a certain amount of immunity is provided to those who cannot receive that vaccine.

HORMONE: A substance in the body that acts like a messenger. It can move from one organ to another, giving signals to help control how different organs work.

HYDRATED: When the body has enough water to function well.

HYDROGEN: The simplest and lightest element that, when alone, is a gas. Two hydrogens can bind with one oxygen to make water (H_2O). Water can be a solid (ice), liquid (water), or gas (steam).

IBUPROFEN: Commonly known as either Advil or Motrin, a medication used to help bring fevers down or to treat headaches or body aches.

IMMUNE SYSTEM: A group of important areas of the body, including lymph nodes and tonsils, that help fight infection.

IMMUNITY: An individual's ability to resist getting a certain infection when exposed to that illness. This can be due to having gotten a certain illness, or, more effectively, after receiving a vaccine.

IMMUNOLOGIST: A person whose work focuses on learning about the immune system.

INSULIN: A hormone produced by the pancreas that helps regulate glucose (a type of sugar) levels in the body.

INTESTINES: A long continuous tube running from the stomach to the anus (where poop comes out). It helps to absorb nutrients for energy and growth, and also helps to move waste to be removed from the body.

JOINT: A structure in the body located between two bones, which allows movement in several directions (knee, elbow, wrist, etc.).

KIDNEY: An organ (most commonly two kidneys) located inside the lower back area that help filter the blood of waste substances. The kidneys turn blood's waste products into urine.

LARGE INTESTINES: The last/second part of the intestines. They are about five feet long, and three inches in diameter. They help to absorb water from food and drinks, and are the last tube that food and waste pass through before the waste portion of food comes out as poop.

METABOLISM: The process of the body turning food into energy.

MICELLE: Soap molecules arrange themselves in tiny clusters called micelles. They form a circle, with the water-loving ends on the outer part of the circle and the oil-loving ends on the inner part of the circle.

MINERAL: An element found in foods that is essential for health (for example, calcium, phosphorus, potassium, iron, or magnesium).

MOLECULE: A substance made up of two or more atoms (or elements). For example, water (H_2O) or carbon dioxide (CO_2).

MUSCLE: A structure in the body that provides movement, strength, and balance. Most muscles are attached to joints, and bones.

NERVE: A fiber made up of neurons that transmits signals and information all over the body.

NEURON: A special type of cell in the nervous system that transmits nerve impulses.

NEUTRALIZE: When referring to acids and bases, neutralizing balances these out, where if you mix something alkaline (basic) and something acidic, the substance can be neutralized to be similar to water.

NITROGEN: An element that is a gas, and is the most plentiful element on earth. It is present in proteins as well as in genetic material of our cells.

NONDOMINANT: Related to handedness, the less-used hand (or foot). For example, the left hand is nondominant in a right-handed person.

OXYGEN: The most important element for our respiration/breathing. The element most important to provide energy through our bloodstream to all of our cells and our lungs. When combined with two hydrogens, it forms water (H2O).

PANCREAS: A large organ near the stomach that helps with digestion as well as in regulating sugar content in the body.

PORES: Tiny holes throughout all of the skin that allow for tiny droplets of water and salt (sweat) to come out when you are hot.

POTASSIUM: An element/mineral necessary in the diet. Found in bananas, sweet potatoes, and broccoli.

PRESCRIBE/PRESCRIPTION: Instructions given by a doctor regarding a specific medicine to take—this includes how much to take, how often, and for how long. (For instance; "Take two teaspoons two times each day for seven days.")

PROTEIN: A nutrient needed for growth. Proteins are found in most cells in the body, and are made up of many amino acids (see definition for amino acid). Proteins are in foods such as meat, beans, chicken, eggs, fish, and nuts. Proteins in the body include enzymes, hormones, and antibodies.

RECTUM/ANUS: The lowest/last parts of the large intestines that store waste (poop) before it is expelled from the body.

REM: "Rapid Eye Movement," or the deepest stage of sleep, where the eyes move back and forth very rapidly (while still closed). Dreams take place in this stage.

SALIVA: The liquid in the mouth, produced by salivary glands. Saliva helps with eating by moistening food. It also contains substances (enzymes) which help with digestion.

SMALL INTESTINES: The first part of the intestines, beginning right after the stomach. The small intestines are about one inch in diameter, and about 22 feet long.

SOAP MOLECULE: A long molecule made up of a combination of fatty acids and salts and a long 'tail' made up of hydrogens and carbons. One end is 'water loving' and the other end is 'oil loving.'

SPINAL CORD: A long bundle of nerve fibers that travels from the bottom of the brain to the lower back, protected by the vertebrae (back bones). It acts to transmit information from the brain to the nerves all over the body.

STARCH: A type of carbohydrate that is a larger molecule than sugar, but otherwise very similar. It contains carbon, hydrogen, and oxygen, and is in foods such as breads, corn, rice, and cereal.

STOMACH: The sac-like structure, which is partly muscle and is lined with material to help digestion, where food is broken down into smaller pieces before it moves on to the intestines.

STRENGTH: The ability to generate physical power, such as lifting, pushing, or throwing.

STRESS: What you feel when you are worried or uncomfortable about something.

SULFUR: An element that is essential in making proteins.

SUPPOSITORY: A medication administered in the anus (bottom), which usually works the same way as a pill taken by mouth works.

SYRINGE: The plastic container that contains the material in a vaccine.

URINE: The liquid substance made of water and waste products from the blood that comes out by passing from the kidneys to the bladder to the potty.

VACCINE: A substance administered, usually by a shot, to trigger a person's immune system to make blockers (antibodies) against an infection.

VIRUS: A substance that causes infections. It is too small to even be seen under a microscope, and is made of tiny molecules and a protective coat of protein.

VITAMIN: A compound necessary for growth that is usually required in very small quantities in the diet because they can't be made by the body. There are 13 all together: Vitamins A, C, E, D, K and the B-vitamins (thiamine, riboflavin, niacin, pantothenic acid, biotin, B6, B12, and folate).

VITAMIN A: A vitamin necessary in the diet that helps with vision. Commonly found in carrots, milk, and cheese.

VITAMIN B: (Folate/Folic Acid) A vitamin necessary in the diet, found in spinach and meat. Important for strong cells and healthy blood.

VITAMIN C: A vitamin necessary in the diet, which helps make a strong immune system and helps with healing. Found in citrus fruits and dark green vegetables.

VITAMIN D: A vitamin necessary in the diet that helps with bone strength. It can partly be made in the body with the help of sunlight, and can be found in foods such as milk and cheese.

WASTE: Material that leaves the body because it is not needed for nutrition. This includes pee (urine) and poop (feces).

WATER: An essential nutrient made up of two hydrogen atoms and one oxygen atom (H_2O). Important for all functions of the body, including digestion, joint health, and kidney function. Up to 60% of the human body is made of water.

ABOUT THE AUTHOR

Dr. Nina Shapiro has been taking care of children for nearly twenty-five years, as a professor and director of Pediatric Ear, Nose, and Throat Surgery at the Mattel Children's Hospital UCLA. She has written and edited several books, including *Take a Deep Breath: Clear the Air for the Health of Your Child*, *50 Studies Every Pediatrician Should Know*, and *HYPE: A Doctor's Guide to Medical Myths, Exaggerated Claims and Bad Advice: How to Tell What's Real and What's Not*, which was a Publisher's Weekly "Best Book of 2018." Her work has appeared in *The Wall Street Journal*, *The Washington Post*, CNN, NPR, and she is a regular guest on *The Doctors* TV show.

She lives in Los Angeles with her husband, who's also a surgeon, and their children, who teach their doctor parents something every day. For additional information on events and projects, please see drninashapiro.com, or follow her @drninashapiro on Twitter and Instagram.

ABOUT THE ILLUSTRATOR

Nicole Grimes is a graduate of the Loyola Marymount University School of Film and Television, where she was a Presidential Scholar and animation major. She illustrated *The Ultimate College Student Health Handbook: Your Guide for Everything from Hangovers to Homesickness* (Skyhorse, 2020), and previously illustrated for Tsehai Publishing. Nicole's background in dance and musical theater fuels her passion for 2D animation, story boarding, and visual choreography. For additional projects and information, please see https://www.nicolecg.com.

RECOMMENDED READING

Love learning about science and health? Here are a few other sites and books you might want to check out!

Websites

Kids Health.org

https://kidshealth.org/en/kids/stay-healthy/?WT.
   ac=k-nav-stay-healthy

Nutrition.gov

https://www.nutrition.gov/topics/nutrition-age/
   children/kids-corner

PBS Kids.org

https://pbskids.org/video/sid-science-kid/1568872094

Books

The Body Image Book for Girls by Charlotte H. Markey, PhD

The Body Image Book for Boys by Charlotte H. Markey, PhD

The Care & Keeping of You: The Body Book for Younger Girls by Valorie Schefer

Guy Stuff: The Body Book for Boys by Cara Natterson

From Chewing to Pooing: Food's Journey Through Your Body to Potty by Lauren Gehringer and Dr. Natalie Gehringer

Mindful Games: Sharing Mindfulness and Meditation with Children, Teens, and Families by Susan Kaiser Greenland and Annaka Harris

My First Human Body Book by Patricia J. Wynne and Donald M. Silver

INDEX